Scary Dairy, Wild Wheat and Coping with E's

A dietary approach to children's behavioural problems through diet

Tessa Lobb

Scary Dairy, Wild Wheat and Coping with E's

A dietary approach to children's behavioural problems through diet

Tessa Lobb

Grub Street • London

Published in 2005 by
Grub Street
4 Rainham Close
London
SW11 6SS
Email: food@grubstreet.co.uk
Web: www.grubstreet.co.uk

Text copyright © Tessa Lobb 2005
Copyright this edition © Grub Street 2005
Designed by Lizzie Ballantyne
Cover photographs Michelle Garrett

British Library Cataloguing in Publication Data
Lobb, Tessa
Scary dairy, wild wheat and coping with E's: a practical approach to children's
behavioural problems through diet
1. Attention-deficit hyperactivity disorder - Diet therapy - Popular works
2. Attention -deficit-disordered children - Behaviour modification - Popular works
I. Title
618.9'28589'0654

ISBN-10 : 1904943 28 4

Printed and bound in India

CONTENTS

INTRODUCTION

If you are concerned that your child's behaviour
is a problem, and are wondering whether they have
ADHD (Attention Deficit Hyperactivity Disorder),
then read on.

There has been a considerable amount of media coverage on the subject of ADHD. Children with this condition have overactive and impulsive behaviour and find it difficult to concentrate, to the extent that it is a problem socially, in school and at home. Research has found that it is more common in boys than girls and that 30 to 40 per cent grow out of it by the time they reach adulthood. ADHD has nothing to do with intellect. A bright child could still have ADHD.

Problems may arise if your child constantly displays these patterns of behaviour at home, at school and socially at an inappropriate level, when compared to other children of a similar age:
- Has high energy levels, compared to their peers and runs you ragged
- Acts without thinking about the consequences to themselves or others
- Has a short attention span, difficulty in understanding and/or completing a task
- Forgetful
- Can't sit still – always fidgets and fiddles
- Easily distracted and is a distraction to others
- Talks nonstop and interrupts others
- Has difficulty making friends
- Easily led or 'set up' by others
- Aggressive

When you compare your child's behaviour with other children, take into account that we all have different standards and we should keep what we think is good behaviour in perspective. The list above could apply to any child. It is the degree to which they display these behaviours that should be considered. You might feel that your child has a problem, but not to the extent that they have ADHD.

Medication such as Ritalin can be prescribed, but can cause side effects such as sleep problems, weight loss, and depression. We also do not know the long term effects of the drug. Children have to be regularly monitored, and must also have support at home and at school. Although drugs such as

Ritalin can be extremely helpful to some children, research has shown that about 30 per cent of ADHD children do not benefit from taking such drugs to control their behaviour.

Although it is difficult to test the effects of diet on behaviour, there is evidence that some children with ADHD react to certain foods, particularly dairy products and food additives. Research with boys has shown that preservatives and food colourings could be linked with hyperactivity and attention difficulties. There is not enough evidence yet to tell us how many children would benefit from a change of diet, but it is worth trying as long as it is discussed with your GP first. A leaflet issued by the Mental Health Foundation entitled 'All About ADHD' confirms this theory.

Recent research has suggested that a high proportion of children suffering from ADHD had abnormally low iron levels. After a month of taking iron supplements, the hyperactive symptoms appeared to improve. It was stressed that an excess of iron can be harmful and recommended that levels should be assessed, before considering supplements, and that attention should be taken to include iron rich foods such as red meat, nuts and seeds.

A deficiency of zinc has also been known to exist in some children. Again, red meat, nuts, seeds and seafood are high in zinc and should be included in your child's diet.

The media have blamed poor diet for ADHD, and to a certain extent I agree. However, prior to realising my son was intolerant to wheat, dairy and E numbers, he had quite a healthy balanced diet. Junk food was kept to the minimum and no excess sugar. The intolerance appears to be the key to overcoming the behaviour problems.

Alex, my son, the inspiration for this book, displayed all the behaviours, to the extent that it was a problem in school and at home. Compared with other children, his behaviour fell short of the norm. He was, and still is, very bright for his age. I discovered that the problems in behaviour were due mainly to a wheat and dairy intolerance and too many E numbers.

A wheat intolerance means that you cannot eat any food containing wheat or wheat derivatives, but can still eat foods containing oats, barley and rye, as opposed to a gluten intolerance where you have problems with all types of grain.

A dairy intolerance is a reaction to anything which contains milk or milk derivatives, most commonly, cow's milk. Sometimes goat's or ewe's milk can be tolerated. My son can take goat's milk, but is not particularly enthusiastic about the taste.

Prior to implementing the diet, my son was over active and over reactive, to the extent that his behaviour was being increasingly criticised and commented upon.

After eliminating wheat and dairy from his diet, Alex's behaviour improved drastically. He is still lively, but the aggression and mood swings are far less apparent. His concentration has improved and he does not fiddle and fidget as much as he used to.

The wheat-free and dairy-free diet books I have read contain recipes that make an already ostracised child (because of their behaviour) feel even more isolated when they have to eat what the average child would consider as 'strange food'. Children don't like to be different. These books do not set out the basics to make it easy for the average parent to follow, or even consider how to put it into practice. Some of the ingredients used prove expensive for families on a tight budget.

A friend commented on the way we managed my son's diet; making it child friendly, using a commonsense approach and a little bit of imagination. She said that I should share it...so here goes.

Nowadays, many mothers go out to work, either out of necessity, or to have those little extras. There is nothing wrong with that, I work full time. The last thing we feel like doing when we get home is slaving away in a hot kitchen preparing food for the family. Supermarkets have thought of us and enticed us into buying ready-prepared meals that we can just pop in the oven for 20 minutes or even quicker, into a microwave. The family can choose what they want – they need not have the same meal – it stops any arguments!

Children are taught a little about nutrition in school, but unless they are a budding 'Delia' or 'Jamie', they need not concern themselves too much about food, because supermarkets can cater to their needs without all the hassle.

This situation has been going on for the last twenty or thirty years and now we are starting to pay the price. The so-called 'healthy options' usually aren't: low fat usually means high sugar, no added sugar means loaded with artificial sweeteners or fat and the list of additives is enough to make you ill, just reading the label.

Let's concentrate on children, because that is what this book is about. Ask yourself:
- How many children do you know who suffer from asthma?
- How many children with eczema?
- How many have unhealthy complexions?
- How many with allergies?
- How many children have you noticed whose front teeth have eroded through drinking fizzy, sugary drinks?
- How many can eat a tube of Smarties without getting hyperactive?
- What do you think about obesity in children?

- Why are behavioural problems on the increase?

It's a little worrying to say the least, isn't it? All these problems are on the increase and I believe that most are related to diet.

More enlightened doctors have been telling us for some considerable time that eczema and asthma can be irritated by certain foods, in particular, wheat, dairy and additives. We have been warned about too much sugar eroding teeth and the increase of childhood diabetes and diabetes later in life. Do we really listen?

We are aware that additives, colourings and preservatives found in most processed foods have been linked to hyperactivity in children. I firmly believe that another cause can be an intolerance to dairy and/or wheat. There have been studies which suggest that some children may be intolerant to pesticides, sprayed on crops, and thus absorbed by the grains, fruits and vegetables.

If you have tried cutting out E numbers and your child is still having behaviour problems, consider cutting out wheat and dairy too.

I did with my son, and it worked.

There are several theories about why children, and adults, for that matter, become intolerant to foodstuffs.

It has been said that antibiotics can kill off the 'good bugs' in the gut, thus causing an intolerance to certain foods, in particular, wheat and dairy. The most common reactions we hear about are asthma or eczema, but I am convinced that my son is not the only child to suffer with behavioural problems as a result of a wheat and dairy intolerance. For all we know, this could be happening to adults too.

I believe, as do many others, that colourings, additives and preservatives in today's foods are responsible for a high proportion of behavioural problems. A growing number of nutritionists and doctors now recognise this and have reported on how schools have lowered hyperactivity in children by cutting out 'junk' foods. We still do not know what harm these chemicals may do in later life.

As all the experts have been telling us, we should eat more fresh foods and steer clear of additives found in processed foods. Ideally all food should be organic, but I think Utopia is a long way off. We've got to get back in the kitchen and back to the basics!

Parents will spend money on child psychologists, have their child put on medication, diagnosed as suffering from Attention Deficit Hyperactivity Disorder (ADHD or ADD without hyperactivity), rather than trying to adopt an alternative healthier eating regime. As you are reading this book, I would like to think that you do not fall into that category and that you wouldn't mind a little inconvenience when considering the welfare of your child.

If you saw a child who was grossly overweight, you would probably be disgusted with the parents for being so irresponsible and feel like reporting them to the NSPCC. I know I would. If you saw a child that looked malnourished you would think exactly the same. You would feel sorry for a child whose skin was cracked and bleeding through eczema and be concerned if a child suffered with asthma.

Nobody cares about a child with behavioural problems, unless they are directly involved. But they are all connected in many cases by diet. The symptoms just come out in a different way.

So there is no mystery or revelation to this diet. It is purely wheat, dairy and additive free. Why not give it a try?

I have kept the recipes as plain and simple as I can. I've taken away the initial hard work. You will find a list of basics for your store cupboard to get you started, plus adapted recipes for every day meals that children would be familiar with, but with a healthy touch.

All of the recipes in this book enable modern families, used to eating convenience foods to get into the habit of cooking wholesome family food.

Parents on tight budgets might even find that they save some money on food bills. You may find that although your child is intolerant to colourings, additives and preservatives, they can tolerate wheat and dairy. My book will still help you get back to basics.

I'm not going to say it's easy, but surely, if it works, it's worth that extra effort for your child's sake. Once you relax into coping with the diet, it becomes more of a way of life, like second nature rather than a trial. Your whole family will benefit. My partner and I still include wheat and dairy in our diet, but we often all eat the same and feel better for it.

I am not a doctor or a nutritionist. I am not medically qualified in any way. But I am a mother and I can tell you that this diet works for my child and that's good enough for me. He cannot be the only child who has a behavioural problem due to wheat and dairy intolerance. How many children have been prescribed drugs unnecessarily, when they could have just modified their diet? I am not saying that this is a cure for all children with behavioural problems, but surely it is worth a try, and above all, you owe it to your child.

I hope it works for you and your child.

ALEX

From an early age, my son has always been very energetic, very bright and had a runny nose. I thought at first he was tiring me out because I was an older mum (I was almost 42 when Alex was born), but the nursery said he was a live wire — but no behaviour problems to worry about. He woke up at 6.30am and didn't stop until about 7.30pm, when he would fall asleep — just like switching off a light.

I mentioned the runny nose to my GP who advised, 'Some kids are snotty and unfortunately you've got a snotty one!'

Then Alex had some Smarties and, like many children, they made him hyperactive. No problem – just exclude colours.

When Alex was 4, his behaviour seemed to change. He didn't always do as he was told, a bit willful, but we were told not to worry. We noticed, too that he seemed to have hearing difficulties, got him checked out and found he had glue ear. Alex loves swimming – goes every week and a doctor advised us that if he had grommets fitted, he might have to give it up.

A colleague at work suggested that I saw a person dealing in alternative medicine who had a good reputation and might be able to cure the glue ear without the need for grommets.

Nothing ventured – nothing gained, I made an appointment.

Now, this will sound a little strange, but the more you think of it, the more logical it sounds.

The professional I saw asked me if Alex had a distressed birth, for example was he a forceps or ventouse baby? He was, actually the latter. She went on to explain that the plates in babies skulls sometimes become misaligned at birth and mucus gets trapped, thus resulting in glue ear, poor eye coordination and a runny nose. Also, if a child had been given several courses of antibiotics in their early years, which Alex had, usually for chest or ear infections, it would affect the good bugs in the gut, which could result in an intolerance to certain foods, in Alex's case, dairy and wheat.

She recommended that we cut these out of his diet and it could cure the glue ear. I ran it past my GP who said he could not see any problems, as long as I ensured that Alex's calcium intake did not lessen and his diet was balanced, but didn't think it would clear the glue ear. We talked to Alex and decided to give it a try. It wasn't easy – there were far less products and books available then, but we managed to stick to it, using common sense more than anything. Alex seemed to calm down a little, which we thought was him growing out of the boisterous phase.

After a few months, Alex started school, however, his hearing was still a problem, so we had no choice but to get grommets fitted. I didn't see the point of continuing with the diet, so gradually reintroduced wheat and dairy back into his meals.

That was when the problems really started: after only a short period, we had complaints that Alex was disruptive in the class. He would lose his temper for no apparent reason and lash out at other children. At home, Alex was becoming increasingly uncontrollable. He fiddled with things and could not sit still, which would drive even the most patient of parents to distraction! I made sure that he didn't eat food with colourings or fizzy drinks but did let him have a small amount of chocolate. I confiscated his favourite toys, stopped him watching television, you name it, I tried it. Give him his due, he took his punishment on the chin, but the behaviour did not improve. Alex thought he was turning into a monster (so did I!). When we picked him up from school, parents would give us strange looks as if to say, 'Bad parents, can't control their child'.

I am a laid back type of person, but was reduced to tears on many occasions. I was at my wits end. My partner and I even considered whether Alex should see a child psychologist.

What must it have been like for Alex?

Alex caught a really bad cold coupled with a chesty cough. I cut out dairy, as it is known to be mucus forming. His behaviour improved. One evening, not long after, Alex had a pizza for dinner. Within 20 minutes, for no apparent reason, he lost it completely. He was shouting, shaking his fists, crying and almost purple with rage. He kept running up to his room and then downstairs again, ranting and raving. Nothing we said or did seemed to make any difference. The 'emotional outburst' lasted for about 30-45 minutes, but it felt like an eternity. That was when we realised that the problems with his behaviour were definitely wheat and milk related.

The following day, we sat Alex down and explained that we felt changes to what he ate may improve his well being. He said he really wanted to give the diet a try. His attitude was that if it made him better behaved, it would be worth it.

To begin with, it was not easy. We cut out wheat and dairy and steered clear of processed foods with additives, preservatives and colourings as much as possible. A couple of weeks into the diet Alex complained of a tummy ache. He brought up some mucus. I suppose this was the body getting rid of the toxins. It might happen to your child, it might not. His improvement was steady, and it began to work.

I bought some WF/DF (wheat-free/dairy-free) cookery books,
which were excellent in their own way, very healthy, but not child friendly.
The recipes were not the sort of thing that the average child would find
appetising.

We wasted so much money on products at health food shops to find
that Alex didn't like them. Eventually, I realised that it was better for Alex
to have a sensible balanced diet, without wheat, dairy and processed foods,
that he felt comfortable with and succeed, rather than impose the idealistic
diet in the books and fail. This is how my book differs to others – I've gone
through the practicalities!

Meals that were successful were ones like Bolognese sauce, cottage pie,
chilli con carne and roast chicken, because they were so easy to adapt to
WF/DF. A couple of months into the diet and Alex was getting bored with
his food. He wanted the same sort of foods as everyone else. I asked what
he missed most and the reply was that he wanted sandwiches for lunch,
as all his friends at school had sandwiches in their packed lunches. In fact
his longing for bread was so bad at one stage, he would sniff it whenever
he got the chance! The wheat-free bread in the shops back then was
expensive and not very tasty to say the least. My attempts at baking soda
bread and corn bread were unsuccessful. I experimented with different
recipes and bread mixes and shop bread. Eventually I tried Dove Farm bread
flour and their recipe on the side of the packet. Alex said that it wasn't bad.
I've modified the recipe a little since, and he says it tastes better and it's
not quite so crumbly.

The other food he really missed was chicken nuggets. I thought that
crushed organic cornflakes might make an acceptable coating and I was
right. I enhanced the flavour by adding a few little extras and used chicken
breasts. The result was healthy chicken nuggets which taste far better than
supermarket ones, though I say so myself. They are a definite winner with
any child (and my partner). It's all about using a little imagination.

We review Alex's diet regularly and if there is anything he feels he is
missing out on, we try to find a way round it.

Now, at 8 years old, Alex is still quite a lively chap, very bright, still a bit
willful, but he is in control! He is fit, has a healthy complexion, perfect
physique, and is rarely ill. However, if he does cheat or inadvertently eats
something he shouldn't, his behaviour suffers. It takes a good 4 days to get
the system back to normal. You have to accept that there will be glitches
along the way, after all, we are only human.

BACK TO BASICS

If you feel this might help your child and your sanity, trial the diet as rigidly as you can for a month. If your child becomes calmer, then continue.

Most manufactured foodstuffs contain additives and preservatives which can also have an effect on your child's behaviour. To give the diet a fair trial, try to keep the food as pure and organic as possible for the first month, and if it works, you can consider introducing a few manufactured foods. But remember that additives might contribute to your child's bad behaviour.

If your child has been on several courses of antibiotics through their childhood, or may be just recently, it might be a good idea for them to take a course of Acidophilus tablets to help to restore the 'good bugs' in the gut. They usually come in capsule form (I split the capsule and mix the contents with a little fresh orange juice to make it easier to swallow). Also, a daily tonic rich in EFA's (essential fatty acids) and high in Omega 3 oils has been found to have a positive effect on children's behaviour and ability to learn – but I would like to point out that the tonic on its own would probably not cure the problem. It won't turn your child into an Einstein, either. Visit your nearest health food shop or chemist to find out more.

The most important things to remember:

- IF YOU TAKE DAIRY OUT OF YOUR CHILD'S DIET, ENSURE THERE IS AN ADEQUATE INTAKE OF CALCIUM. (If you are concerned that your child is not getting enough calcium, there are very good supplements for children available at local chemists.)
- USE AS FEW PROCESSED FOODS AS POSSIBLE (the added advantage is you won't have to read so many labels)
- CUT DOWN SUGAR LEVELS
- IF YOU CAN AFFORD ORGANIC, GREAT – IF YOU CAN'T, BUY THE FRESHEST FOOD YOUR BUDGET WILL ALLOW
- DON'T MAKE A BIG DEAL OUT OF IT – MAKE IT FUN!
- PRAISE/REWARD YOUR CHILD FOR GOOD BEHAVIOUR
- STICK TO THE DIET AS RIGIDLY AS POSSIBLE
- IT TAKES 4 DAYS FOR FOOD TO GO THROUGH THE BODY
- CHECK FOOD LABELLING – DO NOT USE ANY FOOD PRODUCTS CONTAINING:

WHEAT
- Couscous, gluten, hydrolysed wheat protein, rusk, wheat bran, wheat germ oil, wheat starch, wheat thickener, semolina.

DAIRY
- milk, cream, butter, buttermilk, yogurt, cheese, lactose, lactate, lactic acid, milk solids, milk proteins, whey, whey powder, casein, caseinates, hydrolysed casein.

ADDITIVES, COLOURS and PRESERVATIVES
- E102 – Tartrazine, E110 – Sunset Yellow, E122 – Carmoisine, E124 Ponceau 4R, E150 – Caramel, E211 – Sodium Benzoate, MSG (621) Monosodium Glutamate, artificial sweeteners, Caffeine, Phenylalanine.

The list is a bit awesome, but you get used to it. You will also find that there are products that you will buy on a regular basis so it's not as bad as it seems.

I found that the most daunting prospect was knowing what foods I could use. Below is a list of basic foodstuffs to get you started. You don't need to buy them all, just the ones which you think your child and family would like or what you can afford and gradually build up your store cupboard.

Drinks
No fizzy drinks like cola, lemonade etc.
- Danone Activ Mineral Water with added Calcium, or any other brand with the highest level of calcium you can find (original not flavoured).
- Tropicana orange juice with added calcium. (Tesco sell a cheaper version made from concentrate, but if you find that it is too expensive, you could always use the super saver orange juice and dilute it with mineral water).
- Pure fruit juice for packed lunches.
- Hi Juice cordials – Supermarkets own brand – look for the ones with the least additives. Don't be tempted by the ones with less sugar and added sweeteners – they are less healthy. Make up with mineral water that is high in calcium.
- Soya milk – can get small flavoured milk, sweetened, unsweetened with added calcium, fresh or longlife, but to some it can taste a bit cheesy. Good for cooking and sauces. If you currently use dried milk in cooking, try soya infant formula as a non-dairy alternative.
- Rice milk, lighter, more palatable can get snack size or by the litre and with added calcium. We prefer Rice Dream. You can also get chocolate flavoured.
- Oat Supreme – I found this in a supermarket recently and the consistency is in between Soya and rice milk and does appear to be the nearest alternative to milk.
- If your child really craves a fizzy drink, try 60% fruit juice and 40% carbonated mineral water – a much healthier option.

Cereals

Organic corn flakes, Rice Krispies or equivalent (but check ingredients), pure porridge oats, and some Jordan's Country Crisp.

Desserts

(use sparingly – try my yogurt recipe – less additives)

- YOGURTS – Best substitute I've found is Alpro Yofu Adult and Junior yogurts (junior is lump free). My partner unwittingly gave them to our friends children and they didn't even notice.
- Provamel desserts available in various flavours.
- Organic fruit purées/pots.
- ICE CREAM*- Swedish Glace is brilliant – you can get vanilla and chocolate in most supermarkets, but in good health food shops you can find strawberry, raspberry, caramel and mocha flavours. If you inquire in health food shops they might be able to order wheat/dairy-free ice cream cones – expensive, but worth it!

Bread, crackers and biscuits

- There are quite a few bread products available, some are better than others, but they are expensive and come in packs of 5/6 slices. Some also contain additives and preservatives. I make my own, which I slice thinly and freeze – a lot cheaper and my son prefers it. The bread tastes different to normal bread and has a finer and crumblier texture, but the children get used to it in time. (See my recipe on page 84.) Asda and Tesco sell wheat-free burger baps – very expensive – but can be used as a special treat. Asda also sell crackers, which my son reckons are the closest thing to a cream cracker. Doves Farm make rye crackers but I haven't seen them in many shops. Pitta bread is now included in Tesco's 'Free From' range.
- Oatcakes – check the ingredients to ensure no wheat has been added. Nairn make ginger or berry oatcake biscuits, as well as the original flavour.
- Most supermarkets stock a range of 'Free From' biscuits, but they are quite expensive. Check ingredients to ensure both WF/DF. Doves Farm sell organic biscuits, some of which are WF/DF (Lemon Zest and Nice and Nutty).

Spreads, fats and oils

Beware: most margarine contains buttermilk or milk of some sort. We find Pure sunflower spread is good – some supermarkets offer their own brand of dairy-free spread. For baking I use Safeway Baking margarine as labelling confirms WF/DF and is cheaper than using spread. For frying and roasting I use sunflower or olive oil.

Pasta/noodles
You can find quite a selection of wheat-free pasta. Corn pasta is robust and holds its shape and is available in a variety of shapes, colour and sizes – even lasagne. Rice or rice and millet noodles are a good substitute. Buckwheat noodles and spaghetti are also available but taste a bit 'grainy'.

Stock cubes, gravy and soups
- Use Kallo organic gluten and dairy-free stock cubes with reduced salt, or I know that Safeway's own brand is gluten and dairy free.
- Swiss marigold bouillon (good for small amounts of gravy or flavouring).
- Marmite.
- There are some packet soups available, but you could also try making your own.

Cheese
- Tofutti Soya alternative to cheese slices (similar to burger cheese slices) in mozzarella and cheddar style – they also do a cream cheese.
- Florentino Parmazano – dairy-free Parmesan-style cheese – available in most of the large supermarkets – very much like the real thing!
- Cheezly (2 flavours) is a solid Soya cheese that can be grated.
- Some health food shops have local brands of dairy-free cheeses that you might like to try.

Meat and fish
- Check cold cooked fish and meats as quite a few contain milk derivatives and/or wheat, especially in chicken and turkey products. The information on supermarket packaging is improving all the time. If in doubt, ask the staff, as there is usually a list of WF/DF products. There are a couple of types of salamis and spiced sausages on the market. Safeway stock a WF/DF farmhouse pâté, Kabanos and a German salami.
- Tesco and Asda sell WF/DF sausages and children can't tell the difference. Check out your local butcher or market, as quite a few have started making WF/DF sausages.
- Most bacon is okay but always check ingredients.
- Majority of raw unprocessed meats, mince are fine.
- Try Scan Original Swedish Meatballs with pasta and home-made tomato sauce.
- Smoked salmon.
- Canned tuna, salmon, sardines etc., but check ingredients just in case.

- Fresh fish but not crab sticks, boil in the bag kippers or pâté as they usually contain wheat and/or dairy.

Sauces
- Check labels as there are tomato, brown, chilli, soy, Worcestershire sauces available which are WF/DF.
- Mayonnaise is usually OK – but do not use the 'light' versions as most contain cream – again, check the labels or make your own (see recipe page 39).

Snacks
- Crisps – LIMIT TO ONE PACKET OF PLAIN A DAY AT WEEKENDS (only ordinary ready salted, not flavoured varieties at all).
- Seeds – A mixture of pumpkin, sunflower, sesame seeds and pine nuts as bought or lightly toasted. You can buy small bags ready mixed at health food shops. It is a very healthy option well worth trying. Some children love them, some don't. Try sesame snaps.
- Nuts, dried fruits: Raisins, dried apricots etc.
- Fresh fruit.

Flour
- Doves Farm flours are organic and in my opinion, the best most readily available flours.
  I recommend Doves Farm Gluten Free Plain White Flour as a general all purpose flour to begin with. Add wheat-free baking powder if self raising flour is required. The taste will be slightly different to normal, so use a good quality vanilla essence when making plain buns, cakes and biscuits.
- For bread making, try Doves Farm white bread flour and brown bread flour.
- Doves Farm also sell a buckwheat flour which has a nutty flavour and is rich in calcium. The French use buckwheat a lot in their crepes and galettes, which is where I got the idea (see recipe page 82).
- Doves Farm Rice Flour is good for making biscuits and pastry.
- Cornflour can be used to thicken sauces and gravy.

Vegetables
- Try to encourage your child to eat as many fresh vegetables as they can, either raw or cooked.

Jams, honey, golden syrup and peanut butter
- Always check labels.

SO
WHAT DO
WE
DO NOW?

You've got a long list of basic ingredients, but what do you feed your child? It's a bit daunting, isn't it? Here are a few suggestions to get you started.

BREAKFAST

If you had a large glass of wine on an empty stomach, what would happen? Correct. It would probably go straight to your head.

Now apply this theory to your child's breakfast. If your child has processed foods with a cocktail of additives, preservatives, colours, and plenty of sugar, let alone wheat and dairy for breakfast, they will probably have a bad day behaviour wise. I call it 'The Sugar Rush'.

The ruling at breakfast in our house is that sugar is kept to a minimum; food and drink are as pure as possible.

Some people think it odd to have ham for breakfast – I just say 'Think Continental!'

Here are some ideas to try:

- Cereal with rice, soya or oat milk or just dry
- Bacon sandwich
- Sausage sandwich
- Ham sandwich
- Ham on a cracker or toast with a sprinkle of Parmazano
- Pitta bread filled with ham/bacon
- Soya yogurt
- Toast, oatcake or cracker with spread, marmite or jam
- Porridge made with water or soya milk or Oat Supreme
- Boiled or poached egg
- Scrambled eggs
- Omelette (use oil to cook)
- Baked beans on toast
- Sardines on toast
- Smoked salmon and dairy-free cream cheese on an oatcake
- Glass of Tropicana orange juice/rice milk/soya milk/Oat Supreme or Danone water – whatever option with added calcium
- Kippers, non-dyed
- Smoked haddock, non-dyed
- Kedgeree (rice and fish)
- Poached dried fruit and yogurt
- Smoothie, non-dairy
- Non-dairy milk shake

LUNCH/DINNER

The last thing your child wants to be is different, so it is really important that they feel comfortable with what you pack in their lunch box.
Plan ahead, I'm not a morning person, so I always prepare the lunch box the night before and place overnight in the fridge.

School lunch box:

- Sandwich: cold roast chicken, beef, ham, sausage, tuna and mayonnaise, egg and mayonnaise, egg and cress, egg, tomato and mayonnaise, tinned sardines made into paste etc.
- Cold pasta with ham, tuna or chicken, peas, sweetcorn and mayonnaise
- Cold sausages and a chilli mayonnaise or ketchup dip
- Rice and tuna salad
- Small pack of ham and some crackers/oatcakes
- Buckwheat wraps (see recipe page 82)
- Pitta bread filled with meat/fish/salad
- Small raw carrot

- Small packet of dried fruit/raisins
- Piece of fruit
- Home-made flapjack, chocolate bun, fairy cake or cookie
- Soya yogurt
- Popcorn
- A carton of fruit juice, a bottle of $\frac{2}{3}$rds fruit juice $\frac{1}{3}$rd Danone water or water
- Soup in an unbreakable insulated flask, if school permits

At home for lunch or dinner:

- Baked Beans on toast topped with a DF cheese slice
- Bowl of soup
- Sandwich
- Cottage Pie
- Spaghetti Bolognese
- Lasagne
- Chilli con carne
- WF/DF sausages, baked potato and baked beans
- Home-made chicken nuggets with low fat oven chips
- Home-made burgers
- Roast
- WF/DF sausages, cold meat or burger with bubble and squeak and baked beans
- Chicken wrapped in bacon, new potatoes, vegetables and gravy
- Salmon and pasta
- Baked potato with various fillings (page 73)
- Casserole with baked potatoes or new potatoes
- Chinese chicken stir fry with rice noodles
- Pork or lamb chops grilled or baked with vegetables
- Bangers and mash
- Creamy pork
- Fish cakes
- Fish pie
- Vegetable curry
- Spicy chicken wings

As explained earlier, we are trying to steer clear of manufactured foods, so the meals would be home-made using WF/DF ingredients. Most meals listed are everyday family meals that are not too expensive. If you are used to using convenience foods, you might find that you even save money in the long run! I have included a few of my tried and tested recipes: some of you will already use similar ones. You can always double up on a recipe to make 2 meals and freeze.

INVITE A FRIEND ROUND FOR TEA

As soon as you and your child feel confident, and their behaviour has improved, invite a friend for tea. Discuss with your child what they would like to eat — don't make a big deal out of it being WF/DF. The aim of this exercise is for your child to forge friendships and show that they can eat similar foods to their peers. It's all about everyone enjoying themselves.

Try turning the living room into a cinema: draw the curtains, cook some popcorn, throw it in a large bowl for all to share and play a good video or DVD. You could even go the whole hog and give them ice cream in the 'interval'.

Barbecues

Great in the summer – keep it simple: WF/DF sausages and burgers, chicken kebabs, a bowl of new potatoes, low-fat oven chips, crisps, rice or corn pasta salad, and a wheat-free burger bap for your child if they wish – jugs of hi-juice cordial, or try ⅔rds orange juice and ⅓rd mineral water for a refreshing alternative. You might consider fresh fruit, jelly, or DF ice cream for dessert.

Picnics

Your child can have the same as everyone else – just substitute WF/DF products.

At weekends, my partner and I usually take 6 or more children and 2 dogs for a country/seaside ramble. Part of the ritual is that half way round we stop for 'snack time' which consists of either ham sandwiches or plain crisps, flapjacks and cartons of juice. The children love it and the positive effect it has on my son, knowing that his friends really get excited about eating his kind of food is tremendous! Buckwheat wraps, with various savoury fillings – are a delicious and 'cool' alternative to sandwiches.

WHAT IF MY CHILD IS INVITED OUT FOR TEA?

Now I know what you're thinking – the diet is all very well, I've made it sound quite simple to follow, but in the real world, life isn't like that – what if you are out for the day? What if your child is invited out for tea or to a birthday party? That's where most diet books fall down – not this one!

When your child is invited to a friend's for tea, and the food intolerance creates behavioural difficulties, then it would be very wise to discuss with the mum, rather than take a chance. Explain that they are on a WF/DF diet and suggest foods that they are able to eat.

My son was invited to a pizza and ice cream party. The mum was concerned about what she could give him. We sorted it out by me giving her a home-made WF/DF pizza, which she cooked at the same time as the rest, and some dairy-free ice cream for dessert. A good time was had by all.

Another friend's mum was making spaghetti bolognese – I slipped her some corn spaghetti and Parmazano and no one was the wiser.

The same mum sometimes cooks sausage and chips for tea. Although the sausages probably contain rusk, it is only a small amount and does not appear to affect my son too much, as long as that is the only wheat he has in the week.

You have to accept that there will be times when things go wrong – just put it down to experience. If your child is accidentally given something with wheat or dairy, their behaviour might dip over the next 4 days. Sometimes it is hardly noticeable, other times it might be a rough ride. The golden rule is for those 4 days, you ensure no other food containing wheat or dairy is eaten, as it will have an accumulative effect. At least if you know it's going to last 4 days, you can warn the teacher, child minder, nursery, friends or family. If you allow them to cheat say every other day, they might appear to be all right for a few days, but the intolerance would build up in their system, and you'll be heading for trouble.

Do not get complacent.

So, rule of thumb, best to go out for tea on a Friday so that if they do react, it'll be out of their system by Tuesday and they'll be back to normal on Wednesday.

WHAT ABOUT FAST FOODS?

However much we frown upon McDonalds, Wimpy and Burger King, children are drawn to them like a magnet!

I used to take my son for a happy meal after swimming lessons when he was younger. These establishments will, if you ask, do a burger plain, without a bap (you could always take a wheat-free burger bap with you) and fries. They can have orange juice or water to drink, and McDonalds also sell bags of apple slices and grapes for pudding. Or, if you plan ahead, have chicken nuggets and chips when you get home.

Our local Pizza Hut does not offer a wheat or dairy-free option, but they will provide the toppings and cook if you take your own wheat-free pizza base and dairy-free cheese.

KFC's I'm afraid are not so obliging: the last time I inquired, the staff could not advise me whether any of their food is wheat or dairy free, in fact, they told me that they had no list of ingredients at all.

Baked potatoes are fine. Ask that they do not use butter, look at what fillings are available and select the safest option.

I asked at the cinema if their popcorn contained any dairy products and they couldn't tell me and the only drinks available were fizzy or bright coloured. There was nothing that I could safely buy for Alex, so now I take in a bag of home-made popcorn and cartons of fruit juice. I haven't been stopped yet. In the summer your child will be tempted to buy ice creams while you are out. Pick the healthiest choice of ice-lolly like the pure orange juice ones (always check the ingredients), or wait and have a WF/DF one when you get home.

DIET LONG TERM

If this diet works for your child, but you haven't got
time to prepare everything yourself, or you want more
variety, you could look at the 'Free From' range of
products available at most large supermarkets and
health food shops, and the range is always expanding
to include cakes, biscuits, pikelets and syrup pancakes.
They are more expensive than the regular products
and will not be as 'pure' as home-made food, but would
probably still have a positive effect on your child's
behaviour, (look out for fish fingers — can't really tell
the difference!). It really depends on time and budget,
but it is a well known fact that a growing number of
health and behavioural problems have been attributed
to processed foods.

Should your child get a craving for chocolate, Tesco and Sainsbury are now stocking small bars of dairy-free milk chocolate and Green and Black organic dark chocolate (check the ingredients) – they also sell dairy-free dark chocolate Easter eggs. Health food shops sell Whizzers (Smarties alternative), chocolate mini eggs, chocolate footballs and bars of chocolate, all dairy free. You could also try Carob as a healthier option. Most mint imperials and some marshmallows are wheat and dairy free, but high in sugar so should be restricted as much as possible, as should all sweets.

Once you get into the swing of it, you can adapt most of your family recipes to WF/DF, or experiment: ask your child what they would like included in their diet and then try to deliver. Sometimes it can take several attempts before you meet their expectations, but it's worth it.

I work full time, so forward planning is the key. I tend to measure out the ingredients for bread and start the bread maker whilst I am preparing the evening meal, thereby not missing out on my beauty sleep, waiting for the programme to finish. Buns and flapjacks take no time at all to prepare so can be slotted in to your regime quite easily.

IT'S NOT JUST THE DIET......

Believe it or not, your child has been going through a similar hell to you. If they've had a good day then praise them. It is so easy to tell them off when they misbehave, but we often forget to thank them for trying – a little praise goes a long way.

Remember too that children need stimulation – go out for long walks, bicycle rides, swimming. Go to the park and kick a ball around. If you are on a tight budget, you don't have to spend money to have fun. Find out if there are any sports clubs or activities they would like to join. If the weather is too cold or wet, think of indoor activities. I buy jumbo rolls of wall-lining paper, it's very cheap and lasts for ages. You can cut to the required length, give them felt tips (or paints if you are brave) and let their creative juices flow. Keep a bin liner of bits and pieces such as empty loo rolls, cartons, bits of fabric so that they can build things. Visit your local library and look up activity books for ideas. Get involved.

Encourage and support them in building new relationships.

Rather than giving material rewards for good behaviour, spend quality time with your child. My son loves reading, but he still likes being read to. I always think the most important time of the day is bed time – and even if your child has been a terror all day – still give them a hug and let them know you care and that tomorrow can be a fresh beginning. Whatever your child's age they need reassurance that you care.

RECIPES

RECIPE INDEX

FIZZY DRINKS
– THE HEALTHIER OPTION

Fizzy drinks are usually full of sugar and/or artificial sweeteners and most energy drinks and colas contain caffeine, too. They are usually packed full of colours and additives (the dreaded E's), so not the ideal drink to give to an already 'lively' child!

Products labelled 'No added sugar' mean that they contain more artificial sweeteners, which might be a milk derivative, so don't be conned into thinking that they are a healthier option, they are not.

Try to stick to pure fruit juice or mineral water with the highest calcium level you can find.

Buy Hi-Juice cordials without sweeteners as they have less additives than others. Don't make them too strong.

If your child really craves for a fizzy drink, try fizzy mineral water, or equal amounts of fizzy water and fruit juice. It makes a much more refreshing drink. Alex is quite partial to 'cider': 50% apple juice and 50% fizzy water.

MAYONNAISE

You can't beat home-made mayonnaise, and it's very economical to make.

175ml/6 fl oz vegetable oil
1 whole egg
1 tbsp white or cider vinegar
1 tsp Dijon mustard
½ tsp salt

Traditional method
1. Put all the ingredients except the oil into a food processor and blend until well mixed.
2. Keeping the mixer on high speed, dribble the oil in very slowly, until the mayonnaise is at the required consistency.
3. Store in the fridge and use when required.

Quick method
If you possess a hand-held blender, place all ingredients in the beaker provided, insert blender so that it rests on the bottom, switch on and hold in same position until the mixture emulsifies. Without switching off the blender, move it slowly up and down until thoroughly mixed.

The mayonnaise will last for up to one week in the refrigerator.

Variations:
- Try adding the following to change the flavour:
  Crushed garlic, tomato purée, chilli sauce, chopped fresh herbs, lemon juice, or a little curry paste

QUICK BASIC TOMATO SAUCE

This sauce is a good base for pizzas, meatballs, or pasta. I freeze it in small portions.

400g tin of tomatoes
1 tbsp tomato purée
1 small clove of garlic finely chopped, or ½ tsp garlic purée
½ tsp dried basil
Small onion finely chopped or ½ tsp onion powder
½ tsp sugar
Salt and black pepper to taste.

1. Put all the ingredients into a saucepan and bring to the boil.
2. Simmer for approximately 10 minutes until tomatoes are soft.
3. Remove from heat and rub the mixture through a sieve, into a bowl.
4. Pour the mixture back into the saucepan.
5. Reduce to the required consistency.

Variations:
To beef up the flavour, try adding:
- A small red pepper, and/or courgette, finely diced
- Herbs, e.g. Oregano, Italian herbs
- A pinch of chilli or finely chopped olives

RICH SUN-DRIED TOMATO SAUCE

This sauce is richer than my basic tomato sauce and delicious with pasta
or as a topping for a pizza. Although there are quite a few ingredients,
it is very simple and quick to make.

400g tin tomatoes
4 sun-dried tomatoes in oil or 2 tbsp sun dried tomato paste
1 tbsp tomato purée
1 tbsp dried soya milk
1 rounded tsp demerara sugar
1 rounded tsp corn flour
½ tsp garlic purée
A pinch each of sage, rosemary, basil and oregano or 1 tsp Italian herbs
½ tsp xanthan gum
1 tsp lemon juice
Salt and black pepper to taste

1. Place all ingredients in a medium sized saucepan.
2. Whiz with a hand blender until smooth.
3. Bring to the boil, stirring continuously.
4. Simmer for 10 minutes and season.

SAVOURY PASTRY

I always found gluten-free pastry extremely difficult to handle, until I came across Bette Hagman's gluten-free recipes. She is American and is reputed to be the world's leading creator of gluten-free food recipes. I have adapted one of her sweet pastry recipes to suit savoury dishes. It handles and tastes more like a wheat pastry, but if you want to roll the pastry really thin, it is easier and quicker to roll between 2 sheets of cling film.

125g/5oz rice flour
100g/4oz tapioca flour
50g/2oz cornflour
1 rounded tsp xanthan gum
150g/6oz dairy-free vegetable fat or lard
1 lightly beaten egg
2 tsp distilled vinegar
2-3 tbsp ice water
1 tsp salt

1. Place the flours, salt and xanthan gum into a bowl.
2. Rub in the fat or lard until the mixture resembles breadcrumbs.
3. Combine the wet ingredients then gradually add to the flour mixture to form a dough.
4. Refrigerate for 30 minutes before use.

SWEET PASTRY

As with the savoury pastry, this is adapted from a Bette Hagman recipe.
I have reduced the amount of cornflour to make the pastry less 'short'.
This pastry is ideal for fruit pies and tarts. At Christmas, everyone enjoyed
my mince pies, but no one guessed they were gluten and dairy free.

125g/5oz rice flour
100g/4oz tapioca flour
50g/2oz corn flour
1 rounded tsp xanthan gum
¾ tsp salt
1 tbsp caster sugar
150g/6oz DF margarine
1 lightly beaten egg
2 tsp distilled vinegar
2-3 tbsp iced water

1. Place flours, sugar, salt and xanthan gum into a bowl.
2. Rub in margarine until mixture resembles breadcrumbs.
3. Combine the remaining ingredients and gradually add to the flour
   mixture until the pastry holds together into a ball.
4. Refrigerate for 30 minutes before use.

HERBY STUFFING

Alex said he missed having stuffing with poultry, so I concocted this recipe which seems to go down pretty well. It's a good way of using up broken slices of gluten-free bread.

6 slices of GF bread
1 small onion, finely chopped
1 tbsp of mixed fresh herbs or 2 tsp of dried herbs
25g/1oz melted DF margarine
1 egg, beaten
1 tsp lemon juice
salt and pepper

1. Grate or whiz bread in a food processor to form breadcrumbs and empty into a mixing bowl.
2. Add the onion and herbs, and then mix in the margarine, beaten egg and lemon juice. Season to taste with salt and black pepper.
3. Either roll mixture into walnut sized balls and place on a baking tray, or press down into a small ovenproof dish.
4. Bake in oven 180C/350F/Gas 4 for approximately 40 minutes.
5. Serve as an accompaniment to poultry.

JEWISH CHICKEN SOUP

A work colleague passed this recipe on to me, and apparently if you haven't heard already, it is reputed to be a cure all. It does seem to ease cold symptoms, but it's also a tasty and healthy soup. Try it out. If your child is not fond of vegetables, liquidise or rub through a sieve.

Serves 6
2 large skinless chicken breasts, diced
2 large sticks of celery, chopped
1 large onion or leek, chopped
A handful of chopped turnip, or other root vegetable
1 large carrot, diced
2-3 cloves of garlic, chopped
3 pints of chicken stock, cooled

1. Heat oil in a very large saucepan and sauté chicken and vegetables for 2 minutes.
2. Add stock and bring to the boil.
3. Simmer for 3 hours, stirring occasionally.
4. Keep covered and leave overnight.
5. Sieve or liquidise, if preferred. If you are not going to use all the soup at once, either microwave individual bowls of soup, or reheat in a smaller saucepan.

TOMATO SOUP

Most children love tomato soup. This recipe is as close to tinned cream of tomato soup as I can get. It's quite cheap and quick to make and a firm favourite after wintry walks.

Serves 4-6
2 x 400g tins of plum tomatoes
1 medium carrot, chopped
1 small onion, chopped
1 tsp xanthan gum
300ml/½ pint chicken or vegetable stock made from GF/DF stock
    cube or powder
1 tbsp tomato purée
2 tsp sugar
A pinch each of dried basil, oregano and parsley
 3 tbsp dried soya milk

1. Place all the ingredients, except for the dried milk into a large saucepan.
2. Bring to the boil, then simmer for 30 minutes, or until the onion and carrot are tender.
3. Add the soya milk powder and whizz in a blender/food processor or use a hand-held blender.
4. Strain through a sieve to catch any remaining tomato pips.
5. Pour back into the saucepan and reheat before serving.

OMELETTES

So simple and quick to make, they are ready in minutes and so tasty.

Makes 1
2 large eggs
1 tbsp water
A drop of oil for cooking
Salt and black pepper to taste

1. Heat the oil in a 24cm frying pan or omelette pan.
2. Beat the eggs and water and add salt and pepper to taste.
3. When the oil is really hot, quickly pour in the egg mixture and swirl around to cover the base of the pan. Gently agitate the middle of the omelette with the back of a fork to aid the cooking.
4. When the egg is set, fold in half and serve.

Variations:
- Add a good pinch of your favourite herb to the egg mixture
- Add Parmazano to the egg mixture
- Fill one half with chopped ham, DF cheese and sliced cherry tomatoes
- Fill one half with grated DF cheese and a dash of GF/DF Worcestershire sauce
- Sliced fried mushrooms and cheese
- Fry bacon, finely chopped onion, cherry tomatoes, garlic and a tsp of tomato purée
- Fry mushrooms in a spot of oil, add the egg mixture, top with Parmazano and pop under the grill to cook the top
- A sweet omelette by using basic recipe and spreading one half with a tbsp jam

PLYMSTOCK PASTIES

The West Country is famous for its pasties, usually Cornish, but the Devonshire pasties are just as good.

For those of you that have never tried a traditional pasty, it is a circle of pastry, which is filled with beef, onion, potato and swede, sometimes carrot, but usually not turnip, then folded in half and crimped. There is quite a debate on the right or wrong way to make a pasty: some believe the crimped edge should be along the top, while others crimp on the side. The Cornish traditionally slice the potatoes thinly, whereas others dice. My partner is half Cornish, so I have to bow to his superior knowledge!

A snippet of history now: when Cornwall was full of working mines, miners wives would prepare pasties for them. They would make half the filling savoury (using skirt of beef) and the other half sweet, for example apple, so that it was a meal in itself. The miner would hold on to the crimped crust with his dirty hands, and discard it when the rest of the pasty was eaten.

Pasties do take quite a time to make, but they are well worth it. You can make them as large or as small as you like. My recipe is for child sized pasties.

Makes 6
1 quantity of savoury pastry (page 42)
225g/8oz braising steak or skirt of beef, finely chopped
225g/8oz potato sliced very thinly, or a fine dice
100g/4oz swede or carrot or both, finely diced
100g/4oz onion, finely chopped
Salt and black pepper
Water

1. Preheat oven to 220C/425F/Gas 7.
2. Mix the meat and vegetables in a bowl and season to taste.
3. Cut the pastry into 6 even sized pieces and roll each out into a round shape approximately 15cm/6 inches in diameter and no thinner than 3mm/⅛th inch. If the pastry is too thin, it will not hold its shape. You might find it easier to roll the pastry out between two layers of cling film, dusted with rice flour so that you can use the film to help pull the pastry over the filling.
4. Divide the filling between the six rounds of pastry, positioning on one half, leaving a minimum 1.5cm/½ inch border.
5. Wet the circumference of the pastry with water and carefully bring the non-filled half of the pastry over the filling and seal the edges.

6. Fold the sealed pastry edges in towards the pasty, making a fluted edge. If you cannot manage this, just roll it in and make diagonal marks on the pastry with the back of a knife.
7. Carefully place the pasties on lightly oiled or non-stick baking trays.
8. Make a small slit in the top of each pasty and carefully pour 2-3 teaspoons of water in each hole. The water helps to keep the pasty filling moist.
9. Bake for 10 minutes, then reduce the temperature to 180C/350F/Gas 4 and cook for a further 50 minutes.
10. Serve hot or with a dollop of GF/DF tomato ketchup.

Although the pasties are quite fragile when hot, they become more robust when cold – ideal picnic fodder.

You can freeze pasties after they are cooked, but if frozen raw, the potato will turn black.

SAUSAGE ROLLS

Most children love sausage rolls, whether at a party, on a picnic or included in their school lunch box. I make a large batch which I freeze uncooked so that I can cook them later to order; saving time and wastage.

450g/1lb of GF/DF sausages
1 quantity of savoury pastry (page 42)
1 egg, beaten

1. Preheat oven to 220C/425F/Gas 7.
2. Remove the skins from the sausages. Sprinkle rice flour on your work surface and make sausages into 2 x 35cm/14 inch long rolls.
3. You want to roll the pastry out thinly, so you might find it easier and quicker to roll it out in between 2 sheets of cling film. Roll out the pastry into a rectangle and trim.
4. Place the sausage across the width of the pastry and cut to fit.
5. Carefully roll the pastry over the sausage until it overlaps and cut. Brush the edge of the pastry with beaten egg so that it will stick.
6. Continue until all the sausage meat has been used.
7. Cut each long roll into smaller rolls of about 4cm/1½ inch long and make 2 diagonal slits in each. The sausage rolls can be frozen on a tray at this stage, and then transferred to a plastic bag or container.
8. Place the rolls on a greased baking tray, brush with egg and bake for 20 minutes.

I often spread a thin layer of GF/DF tomato ketchup, tomato or chilli pickle on the pastry before rolling. You could also add herbs and/or sun dried tomato paste to the sausagemeat.

BACON EGG AND CHEESE TARTLETS

When making sausage rolls, I had some left over pastry, so using a 4 hole Yorkshire pudding tray, I made these tartlets. They take minutes to prepare and vanished in an instant. Ideal for picnics and packed lunches.

Makes 4
Left over savoury pastry
3 rashers lean bacon, chopped
50g/2oz grated GF/DF cheese
2 eggs
2 tbsp non-dairy milk
Black pepper and herbs to taste
A little rice flour, for dusting

1. Preheat oven to 200C/400F/Gas 6.
2. Grease and flour, with the rice flour, a 4 hole Yorkshire pudding tray.
3. Roll out the pastry thinly and line the 4 holes.
4. Divide the bacon evenly between the 4 tarts and top with the cheese.
5. Beat the eggs and milk, season with black pepper and fill each tart.
6. Sprinkle with your favourite herbs and bake for about 15-20 minutes or until firm to the touch.

BACON AND LEEK QUICHE

Looks like a quiche, tastes like a quiche. My son loved it and his friends (and Dad) could not spot the difference – a definite hit and ideal for packed lunches or picnics.

Makes two 15cm/6 inch or one 25cm/10 inch quiche
½ quantity of savoury pastry (page 42)
50g/2oz finely sliced or chopped leeks
25g/1oz finely diced red pepper
150g/6oz chopped bacon
50g/2oz grated DF cheese, such as Cheezly
2 tsp Parmazano DF cheese
4 eggs
Alpro Soya Dream (alternative to cream)
Dried oregano
Black pepper

1. Preheat oven to 190C/375F/Gas 5.
2. Grease and flour the flan dishes or tins.
3. Roll the pastry and carefully fit into it the tins and trim. Be careful not to stretch the pastry as it will shrink back.
4. Roughly mix the leeks, pepper, bacon and DF cheeses together and add to flan.
5. In a measuring jug, beat the eggs and add black pepper.
6. Add sufficient Soya Dream to make the liquid up to 300ml/½ pint.
7. Pour into flan and sprinkle top with oregano.
8. Bake for 30-35 minutes or until set.
9. Serve hot or cold.

Variations:
- Use onion in place of leek
- Omit red pepper and replace with chopped pineapple
- Use 100g/4oz smoked salmon and ½ tsp dill in place of bacon and pepper
- For a vegetarian option, try small florets of broccoli, blanched in boiling water for 1 minute and some fried sliced mushrooms
- Tuna and sweetcorn, using a 185g can of tuna, drained and frozen or tinned sweetcorn
- Cubed ham and pineapple
- Cooked cubed chicken or turkey and finish with a sprinkle of parsley and thyme.

THAI SALMON FISH CAKES

Is British farmed salmon safe? Some say it is, some say it isn't – so just in case (and at the time, the supermarket was selling 2 for the price of 1), this recipe uses a tin of Alaskan Wild Red Salmon.

I tried the standard type of fish cake – one with parsley, the other with dill.

My son said they were fine, preferring the one with dill, but that there was not much flavour and it needed to be a bit spicy, so with his seal of approval, this was the final outcome. Salmon is rich in omega oils, therefore a healthy family option.

If your budget won't run to red salmon, use pink or buy fresh from the fish counter when on special offer. You can freeze these fish cakes and cook from frozen.

225g/8oz peeled potatoes
213g tin wild red salmon, drained
1 tsp Bart's Thai stir-fry paste (available from most large supermarkets)
2 tbsp multi purpose gluten-free flour or rice flour
1 egg, beaten
25g/1oz of my corn flake crumb mix (see chicken nugget recipe,
 page 57), Orgran multi purpose crumbs or gluten-free breadcrumbs
 made from your own bread
2 tbsp sunflower oil for frying

1. Slice the potatoes, boil, strain and mash with nothing added and allow to cool.
2. Add drained salmon and stir-fry paste and mix thoroughly.
3. Divide mixture into 4 and with floured hands, shape into patties.
4. Coat each cake first in the flour, then in the egg and then finally in the crumb mixture (messy business).
5. Ideally chill in the fridge for 30 minutes.
6. Heat oil in pan until quite hot.
7. Add fish cakes and fry until heated through and golden brown and crispy on the outside.
8. Drain on kitchen paper and serve.

SKEWERS OF MONKFISH, BACON AND JUMBO PRAWNS

My partner cannot stand fish, but my son and I love it. In the summer, when he is off playing cricket, Alex and I often go to the supermarket fish counter, where he selects fish for dinner. We both love the meaty texture of monkfish, but any firm fleshed fish will do – look for the special offers.

Serves 2
1 monkfish tail, bone removed
4 rashers of not too fatty rindless streaky bacon
12 peeled jumbo prawns
1 tbsp olive oil
1 tbsp lemon juice
A good pinch of dried parsley
1 small clove garlic, finely chopped or dried minced garlic
4 wooden skewers soaked in water for at least 30 minutes

1. Preheat grill to medium.
2. Cut the monkfish tail into 16 even sized cubes.
3. Stretch each bacon rasher lengthways with the back of a knife.
4. Interlace with 1 rasher of bacon, 4 pieces of monkfish alternated with 3 prawns on each skewer. Place on a tray.
5. Mix the lemon juice, olive oil, parsley and garlic. Drizzle over the skewers of monkfish. Cover with cling film and chill in fridge for 15–30 minutes.
6. Remove from marinade. Cover ends of skewers with tin foil to prevent from burning and place on a lightly oiled baking tray.
7. Under a medium pre-heated grill, cook for approximately 10-15 minutes, turning frequently and adding a little of the left over marinade if required.
8. Serve on or off the skewer with boiled new potatoes and vegetables of your choice.

FISH PIE

Salmon, cod and prawns in a white sauce, topped with mashed potato.
If cod and prawns work out too expensive, substitute a cheaper firm white
fish, such as coley and substitute peas and sweetcorn for the prawns.

Serves 3-4
150g/6oz salmon fillet
150g/6oz cod fillet
100g/4oz cooked shelled prawns, defrosted
220ml/8fl oz soya milk
50g/2oz dairy-free margarine
1 rounded tbsp of gluten-free flour
600g/1½ lb potatoes, peeled and thinly sliced
1 tbsp finely chopped parsley
Salt and black pepper

1. Preheat oven to 200C/400F/Gas 6 and grease a 1 litre/2 pint pie dish.
2. Boil the potatoes for 15 20 minutes, or until soft enough for mashing.
3. Meanwhile, lay the salmon and cod flat in the bottom of a frying pan and cover with the soya milk.
4. Bring pan to the boil and then simmer gently for approximately 5 minutes or until the fish begins to flake.
5. Strain the liquid and reserve for the sauce. Flake the fish.
6. Place 25g/1oz of the dairy-free margarine, the gluten-free flour and milk in a saucepan and, whisking constantly, bring to the boil, to form a white sauce.
7. Fold in the fish, prawns and parsley and season with salt and black pepper.
8. Pour the mixture into the pie dish.
9. Strain the potatoes, add the remaining dairy-free margarine, and mash until smooth.
10. Top the fish mixture with the mashed potato and fluff up with a fork.
11. Bake for about 15-20 minutes or until golden brown.
12. Serve with carrots and broccoli.

TOMATOEY COD AND PASTA

This dish is really quick to cook, in fact, if you have made a batch of the Rich Sun-Dried Tomato Sauce in advance, it will take about 10 minutes; so ideal if you have had a busy day.

Serves 4
450g/1lb cod, haddock or coley
600ml/1 pint of rich sun-dried tomato sauce (see page 41)
A handful of frozen peas or green beans
A handful of frozen sweetcorn
250g/9oz packet of GF pasta
Parmazano and finely chopped parsley

1. Bring a large saucepan of water to the boil with a drizzle of olive oil added.
2. Heat the sauce in a saucepan or frying pan.
3. Cut the fish into bite sized pieces.
4. Slip the pasta into the boiling water and cook for 2 minutes.
5. Add the fish and vegetables to the tomato sauce and simmer for 5 minutes, turning over gently, taking care not break the fish.
6. Drain the pasta and top with the sauce.

Sprinkle with parsley and Parmazano and serve.

Variation:
- Vary the dish by using different types of fish or frozen seafood mix

CHICKEN NUGGETS

As we have been made aware, there are concerns over the quality and content of factory produced chicken nuggets. This recipe is simple and a much healthier option. It's definitely a winner as far as children are concerned. It's the herbs that give it that something extra to the taste. You could double the quantities and freeze half.

Makes 16-20 depending on size
3 chicken breasts
50g/2oz organic cornflakes
¼ tsp onion powder or garlic granules
½ tsp dried parsley rubbed finely
½ tsp Parmazano
1 egg, beaten

1. Place cornflakes, onion powder, parsley and Parmazano into a medium plastic bag.
2. Roll firmly with a rolling pin to crush until the mixture resembles fine breadcrumbs.
3. Cut chicken into roughly 1.25cm (½ inch) cubes.
4. Pour beaten egg into a shallow dish
5. Coat 4-5 nuggets at a time with egg.
6. Shake off excess egg and drop into bag and shake until evenly coated with crumb mixture.
7. Place on a plate ready for cooking.
8. Repeat until all chicken pieces are coated.
9. Shallow fry over a moderate heat in a little sunflower oil for approximately 10 minutes. Remove from pan and drain on some kitchen paper before serving.

Variations:
- If there should be any left over, you could serve it up in the school lunch box the following day.
- You could also bake for 20-30 minutes 200C/400F/Gas 6, but they tend to come out a little dry.
- Orgran gluten-free breadcrumbs or breadcrumbs made from your gluten-free bread could be used as an alternative coating, but the cornflakes do give a lovely golden colour.

SPICY CHICKEN WINGS

Ideal for lunches, picnics and party food and a children's favourite.

For 8 chicken wings
4 tbsp GF/DF tomato ketchup
2 tbsp GF Worcestershire sauce
2 tsp Amoy Chinese Sweet Chilli Sauce
1 crushed or finely chopped clove of garlic
A dash of GF soy sauce
8 chicken wings with the tips removed

1. Preheat oven to 200C/400F/Gas 6.
2. Place all the sauce ingredients into a bowl and mix thoroughly.
3. Brush the chicken wings liberally with the sauce and place on an oiled baking tray.
4. Bake for 25-30 minutes.
5. Remove from oven and allow to cool slightly before serving.

CHICKEN AND SUN-DRIED TOMATO SAUCE WITH PASTA

A good filling family dinner dish, which is quite quick to make. You could make the tomato sauce a day in advance.

Serves 4
1 quantity of Rich Sun-Dried Tomato Sauce (see page 41)
4-5 skinless chicken breasts, cut into 2.5cm (1 inch) cubes
A handful of frozen cut green beans, or small florets of broccoli, or peas
A handful of frozen sweetcorn
Sliced mushrooms (optional)
1 tbsp cooking oil
250g/8oz corn pasta shapes
Parmazano

1. Fill a large saucepan three quarters full with water, add a drop of oil (this helps prevent the pasta from sticking together), cover and bring to the boil.
2. Pour the oil into a large frying pan, saucepan or wok, and over a high heat brown the chicken.
3. Add the vegetables and tomato sauce. Bring to the boil, reduce the heat and simmer.
4. Empty the pasta into the boiling water and cook for 8 minutes. Strain and rinse with boiling water.
5. Either empty pasta into the sauce, fold in and serve, or divide the pasta into 4 dishes and top with sauce.
6. Sprinkle with Parmazano and serve with garlic bread.

CHICKEN WRAPPED IN BACON

A simple family dish that doesn't take too long to do. Chicken and bacon always go well together. If you flatten the chicken breasts a little, by putting them between two layers of cling film and bashing with a rolling pin, it will reduce the cooking time.

Serves 4
4 skinless chicken breasts
4 rashers of back bacon, fat removed
600ml/1 pint of stock made with Marigold Swiss Vegetable bouillon
   with reduced salt or a gluten- and dairy-free chicken stock cube
2 rounded tsp cornflour
1 tbsp olive or sunflower oil
Black pepper
Sprinkle of parsley

1. Wrap a rasher of bacon around each chicken breast and secure with a cocktail stick.
2. Season with black pepper and a sprinkle of parsley – no need to add salt as there will be enough in the bacon.
3. Pan fry in the oil over a moderate heat for about 5-10 minutes until chicken and bacon begin to brown.
4. Remove chicken from pan.
5. Add stock to pan and cornflour mixed with a little cold water.
6. Stir continuously until stock reaches boiling point and thickens.
7. Reduce temperature to a simmer and return the chicken to the pan.
8. Simmer for a further 10-15 minutes or until the chicken is cooked through (when you stick a cocktail stick into the centre, or thickest part of the chicken, the juices should run clear).
9. Remove cocktail sticks and serve, cut into slices and fan for a more artistic presentation.

We usually serve with baby new potatoes, broccoli or green beans and carrots.

Variations:
- Replace the gravy with home-made tomato sauce
- Add chopped garlic
- Use a finely chopped chilli in the home-made tomato sauce
- Try different herbs
- Drizzle with olive oil and bake in a preheated oven (180C/350F/Gas 4) for about 30 minutes

STIR-FRIED CHICKEN

I find this a good dish to get young children used to oriental style cuisine –
they think it's quite grown up. If your child is not that keen on vegetables,
you can either omit, or sneak a few in – because they are different in
texture and taste, you might just get away with it.

Serves 4
4 boneless skinless chicken breasts, cut into thin strips
2 level tbsp cornflour
1 egg white, lightly beaten
1 tbsp sesame or sunflower oil
1 small onion, finely sliced
1 big fat clove of garlic or 2 medium ones finely chopped
½ tsp dried ginger
1 small carrot, cut into fine matchsticks
1 red pepper, deseeded and thinly sliced
3 tbsp WF/DF soy sauce
1 tbsp wine, rice or cider vinegar or lemon juice
2 tsp sweet chilli sauce

1. Mix the egg white into the cornflour and coat the chicken strips.
2. Heat up a wok or large frying pan until hot and add the oil.
3. Cook onion, garlic and ginger until transparent.
4. Add chicken. Cook for 4-5 minutes, then add carrot and peppers
   and cook for a further 2-3 minutes.
5. Add soy sauce, vinegar and chilli sauce and allow to boil.
6. Serve with rice or rice noodles.

Variations:
- If you are in a hurry, use a pack of ready prepared stir-fry
  vegetables from the supermarket
- Try a combination of different vegetables such as baby spinach
  leaves, mange tout, broccoli florets, bean sprouts, mushrooms
  or baby sweetcorn
- Substitute beef, pork, lamb, turkey or seafood in place of chicken

CREAMY PORK

This dish is quick and easy to prepare. It can be served with mashed potato or rice and vegetables.

Serves 4
450g/1lb pork loin or fillet, cubed
1 tsp gluten-free Chinese 5 spice
1 small onion, chopped
200ml/7fl oz of stock
3-4 tbsp soya yoghurt or Alpro Dream (dairy-free cream alternative)
1 tbsp sunflower or vegetable oil

1. Coat the pork with the Chinese 5 Spice.
2. Heat the oil in a frying pan.
3. Brown the onion and pork.
4. Add the stock and simmer for 10 minutes.
5. Stir in the yoghurt or Alpro Dream just before serving.

If you prefer, you can omit the yoghurt or Alpro dream, use a little more stock and thicken with cornflour.

Serve with rice, boiled new potatoes or mashed potatoes and vegetables

HOME-MADE BURGERS

I've found that 'free from' and organic burgers in supermarkets usually appear in standard size but my lot prefer quarter pounders. I was also quite shocked to find that many of the 100% beef burgers contain wheat. This is a very pure and simple recipe.

Makes 4
450g/1lb lean minced beef (do not use minced steak as it's too lean)
1 tsp onion powder
1 tsp dried parsley, rubbed between fingers to a fine dust
Salt and black pepper to taste

1. Lightly mix all ingredients in a bowl.
2. Divide mixture into 4 and press into rounds. I use a plastic burger mould, but if you haven't got one, shape with your hands.
3. Dry fry over a moderate heat until cooked through.

And that's all there is to it!!

Variations:
- Lamb and mint burgers: use minced lamb instead of beef and 1 tbsp freshly chopped mint in place of parsley
- Turkey burgers: Add thyme and a sprinkle of paprika to minced turkey
- Pork burgers: Add sage and small finely chopped onion in place of parsley, or a generous shake of pork seasoning (check it is WF/DF) to minced pork

COTTAGE PIE

You can prepare this in advance then cook in the oven or assemble quickly and finish under the grill.

Serves 4
450g/1lb steak mince
1 onion, finely chopped
300ml/½ pint beef stock made with gluten- and dairy-free stock cube
    or bouillon
2 tsp cornflour
Pinch of parsley, thyme or mixed herbs
Dash of GF Worcestershire sauce (optional)
1kg/2lb potatoes
25g/1oz Pure spread or dairy-free margarine
Dash of soya milk or Oat Supreme (optional)

1. In a frying pan, dry fry mince and onion.
2. Add stock.
3. Mix a little water into the cornflour and add to pan.
4. Gradually bring to the boil, stirring continuously.
5. Add herbs, Worcestershire sauce and season to taste.
6. Reduce heat and simmer.
7. Peel potatoes slice and boil for 10-20 minutes (depending on the potato) until cooked, but not mushy.
8. Drain and mash.
9. Add spread and salt and pepper to taste. Beat in a dash of soya milk (optional). Keep warm.
10. Half fill an appropriately sized ovenproof dish with the meat mixture.
11. Top with mashed potato and fluff up the surface with a fork.
12. Place under the grill or bake in pre-heated oven 200C/400F/Gas 6 until golden brown and you can see gravy bubbling underneath.
13. Serve with a green vegetable and carrots.

Variations:
- Use lamb instead of beef
- Add finely diced or grated carrots and/or peas
- Sprinkle potato with Parmazano or soya cheese slices, cut into fine strips
- For mashed potato, try using a drop of olive oil and garlic instead of spread
- Try potato and swede mashed together as an alternative topping

TURKEY AND HAM PIE

A good tasty way to use up leftovers from Christmas.

Serves 3-4
½ quantity of savoury pastry (see page 42)
½ leek, sliced
1 diced red pepper
16 small button mushrooms
600ml/1 pint of chicken stock
2 tsp cornflour
300g/12oz cooked turkey
100g/4oz diced ham
A good pinch each of dried parsley and thyme
1 tbsp sunflower oil

1. Preheat oven to 200C/400F/Gas 6.
2. Heat the sunflower oil in a large frying pan or wok.
3. Add the leek, pepper and mushrooms and cook for 5 minutes over a gentle heat until soft.
4. Pour in the stock and cornflour mixed with a little cold water and bring to the boil, stirring continuously.
5. Add the turkey and ham and herbs and simmer.
6. Sprinkle rice flour on your work surface and roll out the pastry to fit just over the top of a 1 litre/2 pint pie dish.
7. Pour the pie filling into the dish and carefully place the pastry on top and trim any excess pastry around the outside of the dish. You can decorate the crust with the trimmings if you like. Brush with water before applying to the crust.
8. Bake for 20-30 minutes or until pastry is golden.
9. Serve with vegetables and new potatoes.

Variations:

*   Use cooked chicken and add chopped bacon to the leek and pepper
*   Add sweetcorn and/or peas
*   Add a tsp of dried herbs to the pastry before adding the liquid for a herby crust
*   Try diced pork and use sage in place of parsley and thyme

SPAGHETTI BOLOGNESE

This is a basic sauce to which I add a finely diced red pepper to give extra flavour but this is optional. It can also be used as the sauce in lasagne. You can double up the quantities and freeze half.

Serves 3-4
450g/1lb minced steak
1 small onion, finely chopped
1 fat clove garlic finely chopped or crushed, or 1 tsp garlic purée
1 red pepper, deseeded and finely diced
400g tin tomatoes
1 tbsp tomato purée
A good pinch of Italian herbs, mixed herbs or basil
½ tsp sugar
Dash of GF Worcestershire sauce (optional)

1. Brown mince with onions and garlic in a wok or large non-stick frying pan over a high heat.
2. Drain excess fat.
3. Add the rest of the ingredients.
4. Bring to the boil and then simmer gently for about 30 minutes.
5. Serve with your favourite type of gluten- and dairy-free pasta.
6. Sprinkle with Parmazano.

Variations:
- If your family enjoy vegetables, you could try adding any of the following:
  a medium diced courgette; mushrooms; finely diced carrots; green beans; peas or sweetcorn
- You could use pork, turkey or chicken mince as a healthier alternative

LASAGNE

Lasagne does take a bit longer to make, but it is worth it. I tend to make about 50% more bolognese and béchamel sauces; enough to make a couple of individual portions for the freezer.

Serves 4
Bolognese sauce, using 1lb/450g mince (see recipe opposite)
2 level tbsp of cornflour
600ml/1 pint unsweetened soya milk or Oat Supreme
25g/1oz dairy-free margarine
½ tsp grated nutmeg
1 tsp Dijon mustard (check WF/DF)
'No-Need to Pre-Cook' WF/DF lasagne sheets
Parmazano
Torn fresh basil leaves (optional)
Salt and black pepper

1. Preheat oven to 200C/400F/Gas 6
2. Grease a lasagne dish or a square or oblong oven dish. To make the béchamel sauce, put the cornflour into a medium sized saucepan and gradually blend in the milk.
3. Add the margarine and nutmeg and bring to boiling point, stirring continuously. Simmer for 5 minutes.
4. Start with a layer of bolognese sauce, then a sprinkling of Parmazano, followed by a layer of lasagne. Repeat, finishing off with a generous topping of béchamel sauce. Sprinkle with Parmazano or grated cheezly, torn basil leaves and season with salt and black pepper.
5. Bake for 25-30 minutes until hot, bubbly and turning golden brown.
6. Serve on its own or with salad and/or garlic bread (see recipe below).

GARLIC BREAD: Use a thick slice of gluten-free bread, or a 'free from' baguette from Tesco.
Make garlic butter by blending ½ tsp garlic purée, a pinch of parsley, salt and black pepper and a dessert spoon of dairy-free spread.
Spread thickly on to bread and pop under the grill until the spread has melted.

Variations:
- Use Ratatouille for a vegetarian option
- Try tuna and sweetcorn in a tomato sauce
- In place of pasta try using slices of cooked aubergine or potato

CHILLI CON CARNE

I usually add a tin of baked beans, which naturally sweetens it up.
I make it quite mild, then add some hot chilli sauce or cayenne pepper
after dishing up the children's portions. It also saves time if you
double the quantities and freeze half.

Serves 4
450g/1lb lean mince or steak mince
1 medium onion, finely chopped
1 fat clove of garlic, finely chopped or 1 tsp Lazy garlic
1 red pepper, deseeded and finely diced
1 medium red chilli, deseeded and very finely chopped or ½ tsp dried
    chilli flakes or chilli powder
1 tsp cumin (optional)
1 tbsp tomato purée
400g tin of plum tomatoes
400g tin of baked beans (check label as some contain wheat
    and/or dairy)
400g tin of red kidney beans (unsweetened and reduced salt if possible)
Salt and black pepper

1. In a wok or large frying pan, brown the mince over a high heat with the
   onion and garlic.
2. Drain off any excess fat.
3. Add the red pepper, chilli, cumin, tomato purée and tomatoes.
4. Bring to the boil, then simmer for about 15 minutes.
5. Add the baked beans and kidney beans and check seasoning – add salt
   and pepper to taste and more chilli if required.
6. Simmer for another 10 minutes.
7. Serve with boiled rice.

Variations:
- Try using any or combinations of the following: green peppers;
  sweetcorn; cherry tomatoes; green beans or peas
- Serve with pasta or a baked potato instead of rice or on gluten-free
  tortilla chips, topped with a DF cheese slice and melted under the
  grill

BACON AND PRAWN PILAF

This one pot dish is fairly quick to prepare for lunch or dinner, and easy on the washing up.

Serves 3-4
4 spring onions (or 1 small onion)
150g/6oz chopped bacon
1 deseeded and diced red pepper
2-3 cloves of garlic, chopped
2 tbsp vegetable, sunflower or olive oil
225g/8 oz Basmati rice
½ tsp each turmeric and sweet smoked paprika (use ordinary paprika
    if more readily available)
900ml/1½ pints chicken stock
2 tsp sweet chilli sauce
100g/4oz frozen peas or cut green beans
150g/6oz shelled prawns

1. In a wok or large frying pan, gently fry the onions, bacon, red pepper and garlic for 3 or 4 minutes.
2. Add the Basmati rice, turmeric and paprika and cook for a further minute or so.
3. Pour in the chicken stock and 2 tsp of chilli sauce and bring to the boil, then simmer for 12 minutes.
4. Add the peas or beans and the prawns and simmer for a further 4 minutes, then serve.

Variation:
* Try using chicken in place of the prawns, or a mild curry powder instead of the spices

VEGETABLE CURRY

My sister, who is vegetarian, gave me this recipe. She cooked it while we were staying with her for the weekend, and Alex really enjoyed it. It is a really economical dish, once you have bought the spices, and you can use any vegetables you have to hand. The yoghurt gives the curry its creamy texture, but can be omitted.

Serves 4
1 red chilli, deseeded and finely chopped
2-3 cloves of garlic, finely chopped or crushed
1 large onion, chopped
2 tbsp olive oil
1 tsp each of cumin and ground ginger
2 tsp each of turmeric and coriander
2 medium potatoes washed and cut into 2.5cm/1 inch dice,
    or 6-8 baby new potatoes cut in half
400g tin of plum tomatoes
25g/1oz red lentils
400g tin of chick peas, drained, preferably with no added salt or sugar
1 tbsp desiccated coconut
1 medium sized carrot, diced
A handful of frozen peas or green beans
100g/4oz small broccoli florets
250ml/8fl oz water
125ml/5fl oz soya yoghurt

1. Heat the olive oil in a large saucepan or wok and fry the chilli, onion and garlic for 3-4 minutes, until soft.
2. Add the spices and potatoes and cook for a further minute.
3. Add tomatoes, lentils, chick peas, coconut, carrot and water and bring to the boil and then simmer for 30 minutes, stirring occasionally, before adding the broccoli and peas. Cook until the broccoli is soft but still quite crunchy.
4. Place yoghurt in a pint basin or measuring jug and gradually mix in the curry sauce, until the bowl is filled, then return the whole lot to the pan and mix well and cook for a further 5 minutes before serving. Doing this will prevent the yoghurt from splitting.
5. Serve with brown basmati rice.

Variation:
• Try using other pulses in place of chick peas, or with different vegetables

PIZZA

We've experimented with different ingredients, and this recipe was the most successful. The yeast gives it that 'bready' flavour. You can leave the base for an hour to 'prove', but if time is of the essence, don't bother it'll still taste pretty good.

Makes three 18cm/7 inch pizzas or one family sized one
Base
450g/1lb Doves Farm gluten-free white bread flour
1 tbsp tapioca starch
½ tsp salt
2 tsp or 1 sachet dried yeast
3 tbsp olive oil
Approx. 350ml/12 fl oz water to mix
Topping
1 quantity of home-made tomato sauce (see recipe page 41) or a jar of
      gluten- and dairy-free pizza sauce
4 Tofutti cheese slices (either mozzarella or cheddar style or combination)
      or grated Cheezly
Dried parsley, basil or oregano and dried minced garlic or onion powder
Parmazano (optional)
Olives (optional)
Drizzle of olive oil

1. Preheat oven to 200C/400F/Gas 6 and lightly oil 2 trays large enough to take the pizzas.
2. To make the base, place all dry ingredients into a mixing bowl.
3. Make a well in the centre, add the oil and mix.
4. Gradually add sufficient water to make a stiff bread-like dough.
5. On a floured surface knead the dough until smooth.
6. Divide dough into 3 and roll out into rounds about 6mm/¼ inch thick.
7. Leave covered for an hour in a warm place to prove.
8. Top with a generous amount of tomato sauce.
9. Cut cheese slices into fine strips to resemble grated cheese and add a sprinkle of Parmazano for a little extra flavour.
10. Sprinkle with parsley, garlic and seasoning.
11. Add olives and drizzle of olive oil (optional).
12. Bake for approximately 20 minutes.

Alternative Toppings:
Ham, bacon, chicken, gluten- and dairy-free salami, sliced kabanos (Polish smoked sausage), tuna, pineapple, peppers, sweetcorn, mushrooms, anchovies, seafood, ratatouille.............The list is endless!

QUICK THICK PIZZA BASE

This recipe is ideal if you need to make a pizza in a hurry. It will make 2 individual bases or a large 25cm/10 inch one, or alternatively, to fit on a 28cm x 18cm/11 x 7 inch baking tray.

150g/6oz Doves Farm gluten-free white bread flour
1½ tsp baking powder
35g/1½oz dried soya milk
1 tbsp olive oil
½ tsp salt
175ml/6fl oz water (approx)

1. Preheat oven to 200C/400F/Gas 6.
2. Place all the dry ingredients in a mixing bowl.
3. Pour in the olive oil and then gradually add the water until the ingredients form a ball.
4. Kneed the dough until smooth.
5. For 2 bases, half the dough and roll or press out each half to form a circle approximately 6mm/¼ inch thick, but 12mm/½ inch thick around the edge to keep in the filling.
6. Place on an oiled baking sheet and add sauce and toppings.
7. Bake for 20-25 minutes.

If you want to freeze one of the pizzas, cut a large enough circle out of a piece of cardboard and cover it with tinfoil. Assemble the pizza, place on tinfoil 'plate' and double wrap with cling film and freeze. The pizza can be cooked from frozen after sliding on to a prepared baking tray, but add about an extra 5 minutes to the cooking time.

BAKED POTATOES

An ideal lunch time food or quick tea. If you have a microwave, cook the potato and then crisp the skin under the grill. Alternatively, boil the potato until almost cooked then finish off in the oven at 200C/400F/Gas 6.
Use Pure spread, gluten- and dairy- free spread or a little olive oil instead of butter.

Suggested fillings:
- Tuna, lemon juice, black pepper and mayonnaise
- Tuna and sweetcorn
- Salmon – tinned, fresh or smoked
- Baked beans and WF/DF sausages
- Bacon and egg
- Bacon and beans
- Chilli con carne
- Bolognese sauce
- Non-dairy cheese
- Corned beef hash: scoop out potato and mash up with some corned beef (make sure WF/DF), top with a chopped up non-dairy cheese slice and finish off under the grill.
- Prawn cocktail: defrost some frozen prawns (I find the quickest way is to tip them into a colander or sieve and run them under a cold water tap). Cocktail sauce: 1 tbsp of gluten- and dairy-free mayonnaise, a good dollop of tomato ketchup or tomato purée and a pinch of cayenne or paprika pepper or a drop of sweet chilli sauce to taste. Drain prawns and pat dry with kitchen towel and fold into sauce.

FIERY POTATOES

My son devised this recipe all by himself and insists that it is included in the book. I thought that as he was my inspiration, it would be unfair not to.

Serves 3-4
2lb/1kg potatoes, peeled
½ tsp garlic purée
1 dessertspoon olive oil
1 generous knob of dairy-free spread
Parmazano
Chilli sauce or tomato ketchup
Salt and black pepper

1. Preheat oven to 200C/400F/Gas 6.
2. Lightly oil a baking tray.
3. Boil potatoes until just cooked. Drain and mash.
4. Add garlic, oil and margarine and mash again. Season with salt and pepper to taste.
5. Using 2 dessertspoons, shape quantities of potato to form oval mounds and place on baking tray.
6. Carefully squeeze a chilli sauce or tomato sauce flame shape on each potato and sprinkle with Parmazano.
7. Bake for 20 minutes, then serve.

POTATO WEDGES

Most of the frozen packs of potato wedges in supermarkets contain wheat, so here's my version. You could vary the flavour by using different herbs or adding a little chilli or Parmazano.

Makes 3 or 4 servings
4 medium potatoes, washed, or 8-10 Charlotte or salad potatoes
Seasoning:
**1 tsp each of rice flour, dried minced garlic or onion and
      dried mixed herbs**
½ tsp salt and a good grind of black pepper
1 tbsp sunflower oil

1. Preheat oven to 240C/475F/Gas 9.
2. Pour oil in a small roasting pan and place in the hot oven.
3. Cut the potatoes into wedges, roughly the same size.
4. Put the seasoning into a plastic bag, add the wedges and shake until evenly coated.
5. Remove roasting pan from oven and add wedges. Shake or turn over with a spoon to coat with oil.
6. Return to oven and cook for approximately 40 minutes depending on size, or until golden on the outside and soft on the inside. Turn wedges over half way through cooking time.
7. Turn out on to a plate lined with kitchen towel to remove excess oil before serving.

BUBBLE AND SQUEAK

This recipe is an excellent way of getting youngsters to eat their vegetables.
    The best way is to cook extra vegetables with a roast so you have
enough for bubble and squeak the next day. It always seems to taste better
with leftovers. You don't need to use any oil, as there will already be fat
from the roast potatoes. Use oil if you have boiled all the vegetables.

Serves 4
Approximately 1kg/2lb of any combination of leftover vegetables, but
    mainly roast potatoes and greens (cabbage, sprouts, spring greens,
    broccoli, beans or peas), also carrots, parsnip, swede or turnip
Salt and pepper to taste

1. Chop, mash or whiz the vegetables to the required consistency. We
   prefer a coarse mash in our household, but some may prefer to whiz in
   a processor until smooth.
2. Season with salt and be liberal with the pepper.
3. Either shape and press into 'burgers', or press mixture into frying pan for
   a family sized one.
4. Cook 'burgers' over a moderate heat, turning frequently, until the
   outside is golden brown and crispy and hot all the way through.
5. If cooking a pan-sized one, keep turning mixture until heated
   throughout and beginning to brown on the bottom, then crisp the top
   under the grill. Cut into wedges. Serve with WF/DF sausages or cold
   meat, baked beans and /or a poached or fried egg. You can freeze
   'burgers' at stage 3 for later.

ROASTED NEW POTATOES WITH OLIVE OIL, GARLIC, AND ROSEMARY

Now you might think this is too sophisticated for children and I'm using this recipe to fill the book. Definitely not.

I meant to try these potatoes out on the grown ups, but unfortunately, the little people got there first and ate the whole lot! Even the pickiest children rave over them. I can't have a barbecue without them.

Serves 3-4
1.5kg/3lb baby new potatoes or small charlotte potatoes
    washed and dried
3-4 cloves of garlic, left whole and unpeeled
2 tbsp olive oil
Sea salt
3-4 large sprigs of fresh rosemary

1. Preheat oven to hottest setting.
2. Empty potatoes and garlic into a large roasting dish.
3. Drizzle the oil over the potatoes and give the pan a good shake to ensure all are coated.
4. Sprinkle with salt and top with the sprigs of rosemary.
5. Roast for 40 minutes, depending on the size of the potatoes. Give the pan a couple of shakes during the cooking time to ensure potatoes cook evenly.
6. Using a slotted spoon, transfer potatoes to a serving dish lined with kitchen paper to absorb oil.

If you light the barbecue straight after you put the potatoes in the oven, they'll be ready right on time to serve with the meat but you don't have to have a barbecue to enjoy them.

FAIL SAFE BARBECUE IDEAS

As I mentioned near the beginning of this book, keep it simple and you can't go wrong.

It might be an idea to keep a supply of supermarket beefburgers (but with no wheat or dairy) in the freezer that are 100% beef – may be a little onion added, just in case you run out of home-made ones, which should really be your first option.

I also buy up several packets of wheat-free sausages to freeze – be careful and read the list of ingredients, as some wheat-free sausages contain dairy.

Stock up on chicken fillets when they are on special offer and freeze individually, wrapped in cling film and then bagged together.

MARINADES

Classic
3 tbsp olive oil
2 tbsp lemon juice
1 clove of garlic, finely chopped
½ –1 tsp parsley, oregano or Italian herbs
½ tsp Parmazano
1 tsp Dijon mustard, salt and black pepper

Chilli and Lime
3 tbsp Sesame oil
1 red chilli deseeded and very finely chopped
1 clove garlic, finely chopped
Juice of 1 lime
Salt and black pepper

Barbecue Sauce
2 tbsp GF/DF bottled barbecue sauce
2 tbsp sunflower oil
1 tbsp cider vinegar

Oriental
2 tbsp Soy sauce (GF/DF)
1 tbsp lemon juice or cider vinegar
2 tsp sweet chilli sauce

Sun-Dried Tomato
1 tbsp sun-dried tomato paste
2 tbsp olive or sunflower oil
1 tsp sweet chilli sauce

Mix the ingredients for the selected marinade in a small bowl and pour over the meat or fish. Refrigerate for at least 30 minutes. If you want to cut down on preparation time for kebabs, cut meat into thin strips rather than cubes, or flatten meat with a rolling pin, cut into pieces and cook straight from the marinade on to the barbecue – even simpler!

These are the house favourites and can be used for any type of meat or fish.

RATATOUILLE

For children who like their vegetables, this is a healthy fat-free option and a good one for adults, too. This can be used as an accompaniment to meat, or as a meal in itself, served topped with Parmazano or a WF/DF cheese slice – or both. You could even use as a sauce for pasta or for a vegetable lasagne.

Serves 4–6 as an accompaniment, 2-3 as a meal
1 onion
1 small green pepper
1 small red pepper
1 small aubergine
2 courgettes, sliced
1 clove garlic, crushed or finely chopped
400g tin plum tomatoes
½ tsp dried basil
½ tsp sugar
2 tbsp tomato purée
Salt and black pepper

1. Finely chop the onion.
2. Deseed peppers and dice vegetables into roughly 2.5cm (1-inch) sized pieces.
3. Place all ingredients into a large saucepan.
4. Bring to the boil.
5. Reduce heat and simmer for 20 minutes.
6. Season to taste and serve.

PITTA BREAD

An alternative to sandwiches, or use for dips. I use a bread maker to mix the dough. Freeze them individually wrapped in cling film and reheat in the toaster or under the grill. Slit the edge to form a pocket and stuff with a favourite filling.

Makes 12 small pittas
450g/1lb Doves Farm GF white bread flour
1 sachet quick acting yeast
1 tsp fine sea salt
300ml/½ pint water
1 tbsp olive oil

1. Put all the ingredients (wet ones first) into bread machine.
2. Set bread maker to 'dough'.
3. When the programme has ended, remove the dough and kneed lightly on a floured surface.
4. Divide mixture into 12 equal balls.
5. With a floured rolling pin, roll out each ball into ovals about 15cm/6 inches long and 6mm/¼ inch thick. Place on a floured surface, cover with a dry cloth and leave for 20-25 minutes to rise a little.
6. Meanwhile, place 2 or 3 baking trays in the oven and heat to 240C/475F/Gas 9.
7. Remove the hot trays from the oven, handling them with care with oven gloves or a cloth, and transfer the pitta dough to the hot trays and bake for 3 minutes or until puffed up but not brown.
8. Cool, covered with the dry cloth (to keep the crust soft) on a wire rack.

BUCKWHEAT PANCAKES

Buckwheat is rich in calcium and as this recipe calls for buckwheat mixed with water and a smidgen of oil to cook, it is a low-fat healthy option. Doves Farm produce it and you can find it in the larger supermarkets, or in health food shops. Last Shrove Tuesday, I cooked these and my partner thought they tasted better than the traditional ones. We also use these pancakes to make wraps, as an alternative to sandwiches for lunch boxes and picnics.

The French call them crepes or galettes, so if you should be 'en France' you'll find these in most supermarkets, but check ingredients are 100% buckwheat, and no milk or butter have been used. Or, just grab a bag of flour, because they are so easy to make fresh each day. This is an authentic French recipe, found on a bag of buckwheat. I've had to scale it down to a practical amount, because it used 1 Kg and 2 litres of water – that's a lot of pancakes. You can include an egg if you prefer.

You could of course, try making pancakes in the traditional way using egg and soya milk.

Makes 4-6 depending on size
100g/4oz Buckwheat flour
Pinch of salt
Cold water
A little sunflower or olive oil for cooking

1. Place flour and salt in a pint measuring jug and make a well. Gradually beat in enough water to make the batter up to a pint.
2. Leave in fridge for 20-30 minutes.
3. Using your largest frying pan (or griddle, if you have one) set on a high heat. When very hot add a little oil (approximately ½ tbsp) to the pan.
4. Ladle or pour in sufficient pancake mixture, swirling the pan gently but quickly, to make a thin even layer to cover the bottom.
5. You'll see little air holes appear in the mixture. Loosen around the edges, to ensure pancake is free on the bottom. When the pancake starts to turn colour, either turn with a spatula, or, if you are wild and impetuous, flip!
6. Remove pancake on to a sheet of kitchen towel.
7. Repeat until all batter used up and you have a stack of pancakes in between sheets of kitchen towel.

Savoury Fillings:
- Ham: thin layer of ham or a large slice, spread with mayonnaise, pickle, ketchup and roll up, tucking in the ends as you go
- Cold roast chicken, a deseeded and finely chopped tomato and a little mayonnaise
- Hot stir-fried chicken and vegetables
- Tuna and mayonnaise (add sweetcorn, peas or red pepper)
- Sausages, hard boiled egg and ketchup
- Chilli con carne (page 68) top wraps with DF cheese and melt under grill
- Cannelloni: Fill with meat mixture, make a white sauce, top with Parmazano and bake for 25 minutes 200C/400F/Gas 6

Sweet Fillings:
- Lemon juice and sugar
- Strawberries and ice cream
- Jam
- Maple syrup
- WF/DF Ice cream and chocolate
- Stewed apple and ice cream

GLUTEN-FREE WHITE BREAD

I used to use a food processor to make the bread, but then invested in the cheapest bread maker and never looked back. If you check the cost of a loaf of shop-bought gluten-free bread, you'll realise that you'll recoup your money in no time.

There are a few GF bread mixes and bread flours available, but the one I prefer is from Doves Farm. They sell a white and a brown gluten-free bread flour. There is a recipe on the packet, but I've tweaked it a little, as Alex found the bread too sweet and crumbly.

Please note that the texture and flavour will be different from normal bread. The bread will not rise as much, but it is filling.

Makes 1 medium loaf
You have to weigh the wet ingredients in this recipe.
300g/11oz unsweetened soya milk or Oat Supreme
1 tsp distilled vinegar
60g/2½oz oil (olive, sunflower or vegetable)
2 large eggs
450g/1lb Doves Farm GF white bread flour, include 1 tbsp tapioca starch*
     in this amount
1 tsp powdered vegetarian gelatine
1 tbsp sugar
1 tsp salt
1 sachet quick acting dried yeast for bread machines (I use Allinson's)

Bread Machine Method:
1. Beat all wet ingredients together and pour into pan.
2. Add the flour and gelatin, then the sugar, the salt and lastly sprinkle on the yeast.
3. Select the quick bread medium crust programme (approximately 2 hours and 20 minutes). The delayed start or timer programmes are not suitable for this recipe.
4. 3 minutes into the programme, scrape the dough down the side of the pan with a plastic spatula.
5. At the end of the programme, remove the pan from the machine immediately or your bread might go soggy.
6. Wait approximately 10 minutes then turn out on to cool on a wire rack.

Food Processor Method:
1. Weigh all wet ingredients and whiz for a few seconds using the dough hook.
2. Add all the dry ingredients and whiz until thoroughly mixed.
3. Scoop into a prepared loaf tin. Cover with cling film and leave for approx. 1 hour in a warm place to rise.
4. Bake 200C/400F/Gas 6 for 45 minutes.
5. Turn out on to a cooling rack.

Once completely cold, slice quite thinly, bag and freeze.

I use the bread straight from the freezer if making a sandwich for the next day's packed lunch, or defrost in the microwave or toast if to be eaten immediately.

When making brown bread, add an extra ounce of soya milk.

As yet, I have been unsuccessful in making bread rolls or burger baps, but there are some in the supermarkets now. They are expensive, but ideal for a treat.

* Tapioca starch (available from oriental supermarkets) and the vegetarian gelatine help to make the bread a little less crumbly.

FRENCH BREAD

Wheat-free and dairy-free baguettes are available in supermarkets, but some are really heavy and others tend to crumble and fracture when cut. I came across a recipe in an American gluten-free cook book and modified it to use English ingredients and measures. The recipe includes dried soya milk. I used baby formula, which stated on the tin that it was suitable for cooking.

Makes 2 baguettes
1 tbsp sugar
1 sachet of fast acting yeast
300ml/½ pint warm water
250g/9oz Doves Farm GF bread flour and include 1 tbsp tapioca starch in this amount
175g/6oz cornflour
1 tsp Xanthan gum
1 tsp salt
2 tsp gelatin (I used the vegetarian option)
5 tbsp + 1 tsp dried soya milk
1 tsp vinegar
2 eggs
1½ tbsp vegetable oil

1. Grease a twin baguette pan or a baking sheet.
2. Stir in the sugar and yeast into the warm water, cover with clingfilm.
3. Using a food processor and the cake mixing blade rather than a dough hook, place all the dry ingredients in the mixing bowl.
4. When the yeast mixture has about 1.25cm/½ inch of foam on the top, add all the wet ingredients and whizz for about 3 minutes.
5. Spoon mixture into pans or on to a baking tray and with hands, smooth the top and then make slashes with a knife.
6. Cover with a clean, dry tea towel and leave for approx 35 minutes or until dough is about double its original size. Preheat oven to 200C/400F/Gas 6.
7. Cook for 15 minutes, then reduce the temperature to 160C/325F/Gas 3 for a further 20 minutes.
8. Cool loaves on a rack. When completely cold, wrap in cling film. If not being used same day, freeze.

POPCORN

Children will love this. A batch will last a day or two, so you can use in their lunch boxes.

For families on a tight budget, this is a very inexpensive and healthy snack. I must admit that I have smuggled some into the cinema – a lot cheaper!

I've tried cooking it in the microwave, but find the traditional way more effective. There are also electric popcorn makers available on the market which are simple and easy to use and avoid the possibility of burning the corn. You can buy popping corn at some supermarkets and at most health food shops.

Serves 4

2 tbsp popping corn
1 tbsp sunflower oil
You need a large frying pan, or wok or saucepan with a lid – ideally a glass lid so you can watch the corn pop.

1. Heat the oil until very hot.
2. Add the popping corn and cover.
3. Shake continuously to ensure the corn does not burn.
4. Once the popping subsides, remove from heat, but give it a few more shakes until the popping stops completely.
5. It should now be safe to remove the lid, but do not stick your head over the pan!
6. If you want sweet popcorn, add a dessertspoon of vanilla sugar*, or if you prefer, sprinkle with a little salt.
7. Put the lid on and give a last good shake then empty into a large bowl.

* I keep a small container of caster sugar to which I have added about an inch of split vanilla pod. My son also likes the vanilla sugar on fruit.

BLACKBERRY AND APPLE OAT CRUMBLE

We have a small apple tree in our garden, and woods close by, so this recipe costs hardly anything at all, which makes it taste even better. I usually cook, purée and freeze the apples in small batches (with no added sugar). Blackberries will last up to a year in the freezer, so we pick loads, wash and freeze on trays then transfer into suitable containers.

I've written this recipe for people not fortunate enough to have an apple tree in their garden, using dessert apples. No sugar need be added, as the tartness of the apples is offset by the topping. Believe me – this recipe is to die for.

Serves 4
225g/8oz Braeburn or Cox's Pippins apples
    (approximately 3 medium apples)
225g/4oz blackberries
25g/1oz demerara sugar
50g/2oz dairy-free margarine plus a little extra plus some extra for
    cooking fruit
1 tbsp golden syrup
100g/4oz porridge oats
½ tsp cinnamon or ginger or mixed spice

1. Preheat oven to 150C/300F/Gas 2.
2. Grease a 20cm/8 inch diameter x 4cm/1.5 inch deep pie dish.
3. Peel, core and thinly slice apples and place into pie dish.
4. Mix in the blackberries and dot with the extra margarine and add a tablespoon of water.
5. Cover with foil and place in oven.
6. In a medium sized saucepan and under a low heat, melt the 50g/2oz margarine, golden syrup, spice and sugar.
7. When all ingredients have melted, remove from heat and add oats.
8. Remove the pie dish from the oven and scatter the topping over the fruit. Do not press the mixture down and don't worry if a little fruit 'peeps' through.
9. Return to the oven for 30–40 minutes until fruit is cooked and topping is golden.
10. Serve warm with dairy-free ice cream.

This dish is equally good using plums, rhubarb, blackberries and pears, gooseberries etc. You could also top with Soya Dream or custard made with soya milk and a few drops of vanilla extract.

RHUBARB CRUMBLE

This pudding is simple to prepare and just right for an early springtime dessert.

Serves 4
450g/1lb trimmed rhubarb
2 tbsp orange juice
2 tbsp demerara or granulated sugar
75g/3oz DF margarine
100g/4oz gluten-free flour
50g/2oz oats
50g/2oz demerara sugar

1. Preheat oven to 200C/400F/Gas 6.
2. Wash and trim rhubarb into 2.5cm/1 inch lengths and place in a medium sized pie dish.
3. Add the orange juice and 2 tablespoons of sugar.
4. Cut the margarine up and rub into the flour until it resembles chunky breadcrumbs, then add the oats and sugar and combine.
5. Sprinkle the topping on the rhubarb.
6. Bake for 30-40 minutes or until golden.

Be traditional and serve with GF/DF custard, or with soya cream or DF ice cream.

If your family are not lovers of rhubarb, substitute their favourite fruit.

FUSS-FREE FRESH FRUIT SALAD

I pinched this recipe from my sister. It is a very simple and refreshing dessert. If your children aren't keen on fruit, give them a small amount of fruit in a ramekin and then gradually increase the fruit each time. You can also make it into a game: get them to close their eyes and guess what type of fruit they have eaten.

The fruit salad will keep for a couple of days in the fridge. Try out different combinations.

Serves 4-6
1 small tin pineapple pieces in own juice
1 small tin mandarin oranges in own juice
1 small dessert apple, cored and sliced or diced
1 kiwi fruit peeled, halved lengthwise and sliced widthwise
Small bunch (approx. 20) red or green seedless grapes, halved
    lengthwise
Choose from mango, strawberries, raspberries, nectarines, fresh apricots,
    bananas, blackberries, pears, whatever combination, cut into
    whatever shape or size you fancy

Add orange juice or apple juice if there is not enough juice to cover most of the fruit.

If you want to use bananas, add just before serving, as they rapidly discolour.

Serve with dairy-free ice cream, soya dream cream or soya yogurt with a teaspoon of runny honey added.

FRUIT JELLY

All the mass produced jellies appear to have colours, loads of sugar and/or sweeteners in them and hardly any fruit. It is very simple to make your own.

Makes 600ml/1 pint of jelly
6 juicing oranges
Sugar to taste (I use 3 tsp sugar)
1 sachet of gelatine/vegetarian equivalent
100ml/4 fl oz boiling water in a pint sized measuring jug

1. Squeeze juice from oranges.
2. Add sugar to taste.
3. Sprinkle gelatine on boiling water and make up according to instructions on sachet.
4. When completely dissolved, top up to 600ml/1 pint mark with orange juice.
5. Pour into a bowl or individual dishes, cover with cling film and chill in the refrigerator until set. Whisk the jelly when half set then return to fridge for a bubbly jelly.

Serve with DF ice cream.

Variations:
- Use Hi-juice blackcurrant cordial made up with 3-4 parts water
- Use fruit purées and water and sugar to taste (such as: strawberries, raspberries or summer fruits)
- Add fruit to the jellies – take care, as some fruits would prevent the jelly from setting

FRUIT PURÉE

As I mentioned earlier, Alpro produce an acceptable fruit yogurt, but the amount of flavours are very limited, especially if your child dislikes yogurts with bits in.

I found that by making fruit purées and freezing them in ice cube trays, we could make different flavoured yogurts and milk shakes quite economically. You can also regulate the amount of sugar added.

Try using fruits in season or on special offer: strawberries, raspberries, cherries, apples, pears, pineapple, plums, apricots, blackcurrants, – go blackberry picking and get purées for free! I've also used frozen summer fruits. If you have some fruit left over, rather than waste it, purée it – even if it is only a small amount, you could get quite a few ice cubes out of it.

All you have to do is:
1. Wash/prepare fruit as you would normally do before cooking.
2. In a saucepan, very gently, heat the fruit (add a tablespoon or 2 of water if dry) until really soft.
3. Rub through a fine sieve to get rid of any pips.
4. Let it cool slightly. Using a teaspoon, fill up an ice cube tray and freeze.
5. Once frozen you can bag and label cubes to save space.

FRUIT YOGURTS

If I make yogurts to eat at home, I usually use small ramekins, but if they are for lunch boxes, try those small airtight containers used for baby food which are about yogurt size. You can find them in most supermarkets and chemists, and most come with matching spoons.

Approximately 2 tbsp plain soya yogurt
1 fruit purée ice cube (thawed)
Approximately 1 heaped tsp caster sugar or honey (or to taste)
A couple of drops of vanilla essence (optional)

Mix all ingredients together for a fruit yogurt (tastes much better home made). Usually the yogurts take on a more vibrant colour than shop ones – but all natural stuff.

You could also try a fresh banana mashed up with a few drops of lemon juice to stop discolouring, dried fruits and/or honey instead of sugar.

NON-DAIRY MILKSHAKES

We usually use rice milk (preferably with added calcium) or Oat Supreme and a large scoop of non-dairy ice cream. You could use soya milk if you prefer a much richer shake.

Makes about 300ml/½ pint shake
200-250ml/6-8fl oz dairy-free milk of your choice
2 defrosted fruit purée cubes (with some flavours, you might prefer 3)
Caster sugar to taste
A good sized scoop of vanilla dairy-free ice cream

1. Place all ingredients into food processor or blender or into a glass if using a small hand whisk.
2. Whiz until frothy then pour into glass.
3. Serve with a straw for optimum effect!

Variations:
- Substitute 2 tsp cocoa powder and a scoop of chocolate dairy-free ice cream
- Substitute a few spoonfuls of soya yogurt in place of the ice cream and use your favourite combination to make a fruit smoothie for breakfast or a nourishing snack

CHOCOLATE BUNS

Another firm favourite with the kids. These buns do not take long to make, and are handy for lunch boxes and picnics. You could top them with dairy-free chocolate or icing, but I rarely get the chance, because they disappear from the cooling rack. If there are any spare, you could freeze them.

Makes approx 12
75g/3oz gluten-free flour
75g/3oz caster sugar
75g/3oz dairy-free spread or chopped-up baking margarine
1 tbsp DF/GF cocoa powder
2 tbsp soya or rice milk
2 eggs
½ tsp vegetarian gelatine
Between ½–1 tsp wheat-free baking powder

1. Preheat oven to 200C/400F/Gas 6.
2. Prepare a 12 hole bun or patty tin with paper cases.
3. Sift all dry ingredients into large mixing bowl.
4. Add remaining ingredients.
5. Whisk with electric mixer for a good 3 minutes – don't worry if the mixture looks as though it has split a little – it doesn't seem to affect the quality of the buns.
6. Divide mixture evenly between 12 bun cases.
7. Bake for 10–12 minutes.
8. Remove from oven and allow to cool on rack.

CHOCOLATE CRISPIES

Quick and simple to make, ideal for parties and children love them! I tried different concoctions, but then found this ready-made cake covering does the job without the fuss. They have a high sugar content, so it would be wise to limit your child's intake.

Makes approx 15
200g Supercook EasyChoc plain chocolate cake covering
100g/4oz GF/DF toasted rice cereal

1. Microwave the chocolate, following the instructions on the sachet.
2. Place rice cereal in a bowl and pour the chocolate into the bowl. Quickly mix to ensure all the cereal is coated.
3. Turn out onto a lightly greased baking tray (18 x 28cm/7 x 11 inch) and press down gently. If you prefer, you can put spoonfuls in paper baking cases.
4. Chill in the refrigerator for about 30 minutes.
5. Remove from the tray and cut into squares and store in an airtight container.

Variation:

- For parties you could top with Whizzers (GF/DF Smarties alternative) and at Easter you could top with Whizzers mini eggs

DOUBLE CHOCOLATE MUFFINS

If you cannot get dairy-free chocolate chips, try breaking up a dairy-free chocolate bar. The mini muffins are ideal for lunch boxes.

Makes 6 large or 24 mini muffins
1 large egg
50g/2oz DF margarine, melted and cooled slightly
40g/1½oz caster sugar
150ml/¼ pint soya milk
150g/6oz Doves Farm GF flour
2 tsp GF baking powder
1 tbsp cocoa
¼ tsp salt
1 tsp vegetarian gelatine
50g/2oz chocolate chips

1. Preheat the oven to 200C/400F/Gas 6 and line a 6 hole muffin tin or two 12 hole mini muffin tins with cake papers.
2. In a large bowl mix together the egg, margarine, sugar and milk.
3. Sieve the dry ingredients on top of the mixture and add the chocolate chips.
4. Fold in quickly, do not beat or stir.
5. Fill each paper case almost to the top.
6. Bake for 25–30 minutes for large muffins and 12–15 minutes for the mini muffins.
7. Remove and transfer muffins on to wire rack to cool.

Variations:
- Plain: omit the cocoa and chocolate chips and add 1tsp vanilla essence
- Fruit: as for plain, but add 100g/4oz of fresh blueberries, blackberries or raspberries
- Christmas: add 2 tbsp of mincemeat and 50g/2oz of chopped up marzipan (left overs from making Christmas cake) to a plain muffin mix
- Easter: top double choc chip muffins with chocolate buttercream and 'Whizzers' mini eggs

CHOCOLATE CHIP COOKIES

If you like cookies, you'll love these. The recipe contains nuts, but you can leave them out if you wish.

Makes about 24
100g/4oz dairy-free margarine
50g/2oz soft brown sugar
75g/3oz caster sugar
1 egg
½ tsp bicarbonate of soda
1 tsp hot water
125g/5oz gluten-free flour
½ tsp salt
50g/2oz chopped nuts (optional)
100g/4oz dairy-free chocolate chips or chopped up chocolate bar
½ tsp vanilla essence

1. Cream together margarine and sugars. Beat in the egg.
2. Mix the bicarbonate of soda and hot water together, add to the mixture and combine with the rest of the ingredients.
3. Chill in the refrigerator overnight.
4. Preheat oven to 180C/350F/Gas 4.
5. Roll teaspoons of dough into balls. Place 5 cm/2 inches apart on a greased baking tray and flatten slightly.
6. Bake for 12-15 minutes.
7. Remove from the oven. Leave to cool slightly before turning out on to cooling rack.
8. Store in an airtight container.

FAT FLAPJACKS

These are a firm favourite with children and my partner's cricket team. They are very sweet, but I have read that the oats help to release the sugar slowly – good enough excuse for me. Flapjacks keep for a week in an airtight container – if they last that long!

When measuring the syrup, I find it easier if I immerse the spoon in a mug of boiling water first. That way, you get a more accurate measure and the syrup just slides off.

Basic Recipe: makes 15
225g/8oz dairy-free baking margarine
100g/4oz demerara sugar
3 tbsp golden syrup
1 tsp vanilla essence
350g/12oz porridge oats

1. Preheat oven to 160C/325F/Gas 3.
2. Grease a 18 x 28cm/7 x 11 inch x 2.5cm/1 inch deep non-stick metal baking tray.
3. Heat margarine, sugar, syrup and vanilla essence on a very low heat until melted, but do not allow to boil
4. Remove from heat and mix in the porridge oats.
5. Empty mixture into prepared tin, and press down evenly with the back of a spoon, paying particular attention to the corners and edges.
6. Bake for 20-30 minutes until a light golden colour.
7. Allow to cool, then refrigerate for an hour or so (or if you can't wait that long, place in the freezer for 10 minutes) then cut into squares and they should remove quite easily.

Variations:
- At stage 1, try adding 1 tsp ground ginger, or 1 tbsp of sesame seeds for a more crunchy flapjack
- Reduce sugar by 25g/1oz and try adding any of the following at stage 1:
  25g/1oz desiccated coconut and 50g/2oz glace cherries
  50g/2oz dried apricots/cranberries/any other dried fruit that you fancy

I can highly recommend apricot flapjacks.

FIN FLAPJACKS

Alex's best friend Nicholas is a flapjackaholic. Not only does he expect Alex to bring one every day to school for him in his lunch box, he also gets his mum, Barbara to supply him too. Neither of us realised he was getting double bubble!

Barbara has experimented with her recipe and come up with one with reduced fat and sugar. I thought it might ruin the flavour and texture, but it didn't, so I tweaked my recipe with her seal of approval. Barbara – this one is down to you.

Makes approx. 15
175g/6oz dairy-free margarine
100g/4oz demerara sugar
3 dessertspoons golden syrup
1 tsp vanilla essence
350g/12oz porridge oats

1. Preheat oven to 160C/325F/Gas 3.
2. Grease a 18 x 28cm/7 x 11 inch x 2.5cm/1 inch deep non-stick metal baking tray.
3. Slowly melt margarine, sugar, syrup and essence in a large saucepan.
4. Remove from heat, add oats and mix thoroughly.
5. Empty mixture into prepared baking tray and press down firmly and evenly.
6. Bake for 20–30 minutes until golden. Make sure they do not burn – there's nothing so horrible as an overcooked flapjack.
7. Cool then refrigerate for a couple of hours before cutting into 15 equal portions.

Store in an air tight container for up to a week.

FRUITY FAIRY CAKES

Small, light, fruity buns – ideal for lunch boxes/picnics/after-school snacks.

Makes 12
75g/3oz gluten-free flour
75g/3oz dairy-free margarine
75g/3oz caster sugar
25g/1oz mixed dried fruit
2 tbsp soya or rice milk
2 eggs
½ tsp vanilla essence or 1 tsp mixed spice
1 tsp wheat-free baking powder
½ tsp vegetarian powdered gelatin

1. Preheat oven to 200C/400F/Gas 6.
2. Prepare a bun or pattie tin with paper cases.
3. Using all-in-one method, put ingredients into a large mixing bowl if using a hand mixer or a food processor bowl.
4. Whizz for a few minutes until mixture light and airy.
5. Divide evenly between bun cases.
6. Bake for 10-12 minutes.
7. Remove from the oven and turn out on to a cooling tray.

Variations:
- Try 25g/1oz finely chopped dried cranberries, apricots or blueberries
- or 25g/1oz sultanas with the zest of a small lemon or a mandarin

DEAD FLY BISCUITS

Not a very appetising name, but these are my gluten- and dairy-free alternative to fruit shortcake biscuits (we use currants, not flies).

Makes about 24
225g/8 oz Doves Farm rice flour
75g/3oz caster sugar, plus extra to sprinkle on top of biscuits
75g/3oz dairy-free margarine
1 egg
50g/2oz currants
1 tsp mixed spice
½ tsp salt

1. Preheat the oven to 160C/325F/Gas 3 and grease 2 or 3 baking trays.
2. Cream together the sugar and margarine until white and fluffy.
3. Add the egg and then mix in the remaining ingredients to make a stiff dough. If the mixture is too dry, add a little water.
4. Leave dough to rest in the fridge for about 30 minutes.
5. Roll out the dough thinly on a floured surface, and cut into rounds using a medium sized cutter.
6. Place on baking trays, prick with a fork and sprinkle with a little caster sugar.
7. Bake for approx. 20 minutes or until just turning brown.
8. Turn out on a wire rack to cool.
9. Store in an air tight container and they will stay fresh for up to a week.

JAM TARTS

Most children like jam tarts. This recipe makes approximately 24 tarts, but you can always make them with any leftover GF/DF pastry.

Makes 24
½ quantity of GF/DF sweet pastry (see page 43)
An assortment of favourite jams

1. Preheat oven to 160C/325F/Gas 3.
2. Grease and flour two 12 hole patty tins.
3. On a GF floured work surface roll the pastry out thinly and cut out discs with a large round pastry cutter and place a pastry disc in each hole.
4. Place a teaspoon of jam in each.
5. Bake for 15–20 minutes.
6. Cool on a wire rack.

MINCE PIES

For all the children and adults who are gluten- and dairy-intolerant and enjoy a mince pie at Christmas. I have also made mini mince pies using a mini muffin tray and cutting out a star shaped pastry top.

Makes approximately 24
1 quantity of sweet pastry (see page 43)
1 jar of GF/DF mincemeat (most mincemeat is GF/DF – check ingredients)
Small dish of cold water

1. Preheat oven to 180C/350F/Gas 4.
2. Grease and flour two 12 hole patty tins.
3. Cut off just over ½ of the pastry and roll out quite thinly.
4. With a large round pastry cutter cut 24 discs and carefully place in each hole.
5. Add 1 rounded teaspoon of mincemeat to each.
6. Incorporate any left over pastry into remaining dough and roll out.
7. Using a medium sized pastry cutter, cut out 24 discs for the lids.
8. Using your finger, wet the under side of each disc with water and press over the filling of the pies.
9. Bake for 15-20 minutes. You can brush with water 5 minutes before the end of the cooking time, sprinkle with caster sugar and return to the oven to complete, or dredge with icing sugar when cold.
10. Remove from oven, and turn out on a wire rack to cool.

VICTORIA SANDWICH

This recipe is ideal for a birthday cake and no one will believe that this is gluten free.

Makes two 20cm/8-inch sponge cakes
50g/2oz rice flour
100g/4oz gluten-free flour, but include 1 tbsp Tapioca starch
   in this amount
150g/6oz caster sugar
150g/6oz margarine, softened
3 eggs plus 1 tsp dried whole egg
1 tsp powdered vegetarian gelatine
2 tsp gluten-free baking powder
2 tbsp dried soya milk
2 tbsp water
1 tsp vanilla essence
A good pinch of salt
Jam and/or butter cream made with dairy-free margarine and a drop of
   vanilla essence to fill

1. Preheat oven to 160C/325F/Gas 3.
2. Grease two 20cm/8 inch sandwich tins with a little margarine and line the bases with greaseproof paper.
3. Using a hand mixer or food processor, place all ingredients into a mixing bowl and beat at high speed for about 3 minutes.
4. Divide the mixture evenly between the 2 tins and level out.
5. Bake for about 20 minutes or until firm (a skewer/cocktail stick comes out clean when inserted in the cake).
6. Turn out sponges on to a cooling rack, and leave until completely cool.
7. With the sponges facing bottom side up, spread your favourite filling on each and sandwich together.
8. Either dust the top of the cake with icing sugar or cover with non-dairy butter cream. If you are making a birthday cake, to save time, you could cover with ready made white fondant icing and then decorate.

Variations:
*   Try adding the finely grated rind of a lemon or orange
*   Replace 1 tablespoon flour with 1 tablespoon cocoa and omit vanilla for a chocolate cake
*   Add 1 tbsp ground almonds

BEST EVER CHRISTMAS CAKE

This cake is absolutely delicious. It is moist, packed full of fruit and will keep for months. Family and friends all gave it the thumbs up and it vanished remarkably quickly. As an alternative to icing, this cake is coated with a layer of almond paste and then baked so that it has a golden tinge.

Makes one 23cm/9 inch round or 20cm/8 inch square cake
1250g/2lb 12oz luxury dried fruit (sultanas, currants, cherries and
    candied peel)
100g/4oz chopped mixed nuts
Juice of 1 lemon and 1 orange
4 tbsp alcohol (e.g. whisky, brandy, rum or liqueur)
225g/8oz DF margarine
225g/8oz light muscovado sugar
6 large eggs, beaten
1 tsp mixed spice
125g/5oz rice flour
225g/8oz ground almonds
2tsp xanthan gum
1 large cooking apple, grated
Almond paste:
2 medium eggs
2 tbsp whisky
A drop of pure almond essence
450g/1lb ground almonds
450g/1lb sifted caster sugar
1 egg white and 2 egg yolks both lightly beaten

1. Place the dried fruit, chopped nuts, juice and ½ the alcohol in a large mixing bowl and leave for an hour.
2. Double line the base and sides of your cake tin with greaseproof paper. Cut a piece of brown paper long enough to go around the outside and approximately double the depth of the tin to form a collar and secure with string.
3. Preheat the oven to 180C/350F/Gas 4.
4. Cream the margarine and sugar until light and fluffy. Add the eggs gradually, beating well each time.
5. Combine the spice, xanthan gum, rice flour and ground almonds. Stir gently into the mixture.
6. Add the grated apple to the fruit and then gently stir in the rest of the ingredients.

7. Empty into the prepared tin. Using a wet hand, smooth and level the top of the cake.
8. Lay a sheet of brown paper over the top of the collar and bake for 1 hour.
9. Reduce temperature to 150C/300F/Gas 2 and bake for a further 2-2½ hours or until a skewer pushed into the middle comes out clean.
10. Remove from the oven and pour the rest of the alcohol over the hot cake and leave to cool in the tin.
11. When completely cold, remove the cake from the tin, but do not remove the greaseproof paper. Wrap in another layer of greaseproof and then foil until ready to decorate.
12. To decorate, make the almond paste by beating together the eggs, whisky and essence and then adding it to the sugar and ground almonds to make a paste.
13. Preheat the oven to 220C/425F/Gas 7.
14. Sprinkle your work surface with icing sugar and kneed the almond paste lightly until smooth. Roll out to approximately 1cm/½ inch thick. Brush the cake with the egg white and cover with the almond paste.
15. Roll out any left over paste thinly and cut out festive shapes. Brush with the egg yolk and stick on to the cake, then brush the whole cake with the egg yolk.
16. Carefully place the cake on a baking tray and bake for 10-15 minutes, or until it is a golden colour. When the cake has cooled, you can dredge the top with icing sugar if you wish.

INDEX